BIG SHOES

BIG SHOES

In Celebration of Dads and Fatherhood

⌒

AL ROKER & FRIENDS
Edited by Amy Rennert

HYPERION NEW YORK

Library of Congress Cataloging-in-Publication Data

Big shoes : in celebration of dads and fatherhood / Al Roker and friends.— 1st ed.
    p. cm.
    ISBN: 1-4013-0171-1
    1. Fathers—Anecdotes.   2. Fatherhood—Anecdotes.   3. Father and child—Anecdotes.   I. Roker, Al

HQ756.B524 2005
306.874'2'0922—dc22

                                                                    2004060706

Hyperion books are available for special promotions and premiums. For details contact Michael Rentas, Assistant Director, Inventory Operations, Hyperion, 77 West 66th Street, 11th floor, New York, New York 10023, or call 212-456-0133.

FIRST EDITION

10 9 8 7 6 5 4 3 2 1

To my mother, Isabel Roker, who made Al Roker, Sr., the father he was and always will be. To my wife, Deborah, the rock that gives me the support, the love, and the nurturing to be the best father I can be. To my children, Courtney, Leila, and Nicholas, who make fatherhood a blessing, a joy, and a wonderful challenge each and every day. To Willard Scott, who has been like a second father to me. And to Albert Lincoln Roker, Sr., my father. I never forget that while I can't be him, I strive every day to be like him.

—AL ROKER

To my father, Irwin Rennert, who was the inspiration for this book.

—AMY RENNERT

CONTENTS

BIG SHOES

INTRODUCTION

■

by Al Roker

L ET'S FACE IT. WE TEND TO OVERLOOK DADS. Sure, we buy them the requisite tie on Father's Day or their birthday. Maybe a power tool or ratchet set if they're the handy type. But by and large, fathers are down a few links on the family food chain.

First come mothers. Have you ever seen a football player, after scoring the winning touchdown, mouth the words, "Hi, Dad!"? Nooooo. It's always, "HEY, MOM! I LOVE YOU!"

Ever see tattoos on a tough guy that spell out "F-A-T-H-E-R"? Not likely. After all, for my generation, dads were generally the ones who meted out discipline and justice. You tend not to have warm, fuzzy feelings about the person who is about to punish you.

Even grandparents tend to rate a little higher than fathers.

They are kindly old folks who show up bearing gifts, giving extra servings of dessert, and shoving dollar bills in your pockets with a conspiratorial "don't tell your parents, this is between us" wink.

What I hope to do in *Big Shoes* is to get you thinking more about your father. What does the old guy really mean to you and to your life? How does what he did, and hopefully still does, influence you?

No matter who your father is or was, whether a great man or someone who left a lot to be desired, there is something in the man that you can learn from, something that will make you a better person.

I lost my father to lung cancer in October of 2001. He died a little more than a month after 9/11. I watched him wither away and die. I had to mourn him while a country mourned the loss of life and innocence. I realized I had to step into those Big Shoes before I felt ready. Suddenly, I was the patriarch of my family. I didn't feel prepared for the role. And yet, my father had been preparing me for this all along; helping me raise my children, helping me become a good father. How? By just being my father.

To this day, I'm still working on my relationship with my father. I play back certain scenes in my head, moments that define my father, and by extension, me. And then I started to wonder, "What about other people? What are their relationships with their fathers? What do they remember most? What have they learned? How did their fathers impact their lives for better, for worse? How does the way their father raised them affect how they parent?"

So, this is what *Big Shoes* is about. It's not necessarily a big Hallmark card to fathers. What I want to bring you is an honest, human look at fathers and fatherhood over a couple of generations from many different perspectives.

I never thought about the time I would have to step into my own father's big shoes. He was always there to fill them. Then suddenly, he wasn't. Now I have had to step into them; for my mother, my siblings, my own children. I have become my father. I hope that it's not too tight a fit or too loose. I would hate to have to take them off.

My father always kept his shoes polished. It goes back to when he was a bus driver. He was always impeccable in his bus driver's uniform. My mother would iron his shirts and press his uniform pants and jacket, but he always spit-shined his own shoes.

He told me that if a man had unshined shoes, it reflected poorly on him. His shoes always had a shine you could adjust your tie in. Whether he was going to work or to church, his shoes glistened. If he could've shined his sneakers, he would have. And as he climbed the ladder of the New York City Transit System, responsibilities increasing, he still shined his own shoes.

This book represents the big shoes, the footprints if you will, of many different fathers. Some of the stories will be by people you know well, other names may be less familiar to you, but I hope you'll see something of your father in many of these essays—something that makes you think of your old man while you read. And maybe, you will find something that keeps the memories alive.

I guess that's the hardest part of losing my father at a relatively young age. He was three months shy of his seventieth birthday. While I have tons of pictures of him in my home and office, home videos, even a Food Network special that revolved around him and my mom, I'm having trouble hearing his voice in my head the way I used to. The voice is getting fainter as time goes on. Maybe this book is a way to keep his voice loud and clear. I want to pump up the volume.

BRADLEY WHITFORD

■

Emmy Award–winning star of The West Wing *and numerous other television shows, plays, and films.*

MY FATHER PASSED AWAY FIVE YEARS AGO, but if he were able to write this essay himself, he would begin with the proclamation that he, George Van Norman Whitford, has a bright future behind him. Dad's heroes were subversive writers who punctured artifice, like H. L. Mencken and Mark Twain, and even his own death was not immune to mockery.

He was a quintessential member of what has become so commonly known as "the greatest generation." It is a description he would scoff at. As far as he was concerned, there was nothing particularly great about it; you just did what you had to do. Whether it was the Depression, fighting the Japanese in World War II, or busting your hump at work, you dealt with it. The current fashion of obsessing over one's feelings was as foreign to him as music from another planet. He had a clear optimism about the future that only a child of the Depression could have when faced with the abundance and opportunity of America in the middle of the twentieth century.

I was the fifth and last child in my family, born when my father was forty-five years old. It is rumored that my father was not consulted by my mother about my conception. My theory has always been that my brother Dave was the afterthought and that I was put on the planet to keep him company. Once he went off to college, my mission was complete.

Though I came late in life, Dad was the opposite of a fussy older parent. He went on the assumption that if you loved your kids unconditionally and kept them out of traffic, things would probably turn out all right. There was no question that we would be allowed to pursue whatever interested us. He quietly assumed a massive financial burden as Dave and I ambled through expensive college and graduate school careers headed for insecure careers as a writer and an actor. The only repayment he asked was that we do the same for our children.

I always felt that Dad got a kick out of having a kid who was an actor. He would lovingly tease me about being a "ham and a fraud." I will never forget the image of him standing in the middle of the audience in countless school plays as I looked out from the stage, his wide grin beaming as his camera flashed at me. He was encouraging without being cloying and as a result I felt supported but never pushed. I don't know if a kid could feel the same sense of ownership I feel about acting in these days of self-conscious parenting.

Being an actor was a way to aspire to my dad's most joyous

values. The greatest compliment he could pay someone was to say that they were "a character." It meant they were colorful and outside the norm. Even in his eighties, he would go out of his way to introduce me to the animated and toothless parking lot guy he had struck up a friendship with.

And then there were the ceaseless, ridiculous, corny jokes. Dad had the rare ability to make lame comic material hilarious simply by way of goofy persistence. In the years since his death the relentlessness and the subversiveness of his humor continue to inspire me.

I am grateful to have been raised by a man who was so kindly predisposed to the wacky and the unexpected. Dad's life was a testament to the great twentieth-century American values of kindness, hard work, and taking care of your family, but he was deeply suspicious of the herd. He subscribed to Mark Twain's observation that patriotism was the last refuge of scoundrels, and detested pandering displays of flag-waving. When there was a proposed constitutional amendment to ban flag burning, he said that he was proud to have fought for a country where an idiot could burn a flag if they wanted to.

Dad gave me an opportunity that he never had. He was a talented musician who loved public speaking and often spoke about his desire to be a writer. He spent his life working hard, successfully pursuing a business career that he enjoyed, but I often think of him when I'm on the set of The West Wing and wish that he had had the freedom he provided me to pursue a creative life.

After he had a heart attack, my father asked his doctor for

a frank assessment of his future with the clinical detachment of a career life-insurance man. He was an eighty-four-year-old and had a damaged heart. If he were lucky, the doctor said, he would be taken out with a heart attack. More likely was the slow and agonizing suffocation of congestive heart failure.

My father listened without expression.

"Yeah . . . yeah . . . yeah . . ."

There was no sentimentality or emotion, just a frank acceptance of the inevitable.

A few days before his death, Dad told me he was looking forward to a business meeting in Boston in six months. It was a ludicrous notion for a steadily deteriorating invalid who could no longer make it across the room, even with the help of a walker. None of that mattered. He had a meeting to get to.

The very last day of his life, Father's Day of 1999, at the end of a happy conversation I told him I loved him and asked him if my mother was around. He answered with the last words I would ever hear him speak:

"No," he said, "she's a square."

REBECCA WALKER

■

Author of the best-selling memoir Black, White and Jewish: Autobiography of a Shifting Self *and editor of two anthologies,* What Makes a Man: 22 Writers Imagine the Future *and* To Be Real: Telling the Truth and Changing the Face of Feminism.

I DON'T KNOW IF ALL FATHERS ARE unsung heroes, but mine sure is. For the last twenty-five years, my father, Mel Leventhal, has been known in many circles as "Alice Walker's ex-husband," and a few weeks ago he told me people now refer to him as "Rebecca Walker's father." He laughed when he said this, claiming to love this latest twist in the identity game, but I know better. How can I not? I know what it's like to be practically invisible, a living arrow pointing to someone else.

My father, with a rifle and a German shepherd, fought the Klan on our doorstep in Jackson, Mississippi. My father, with a law degree and a lot of chutzpah, fought segregation in the U.S. Supreme Court. My father has fought on behalf of consumers, old people, disabled people, women. My father has worked almost every day of the week to support his first wife, and then his second, and to put his children through college and beyond. My father has packed up the car with his kids' stuff and moved us into and out of more dorm rooms and apartments than I care to count. He has written more checks for root canals and bite plates, bar mitzvahs and baby showers, laptops and trips abroad, than seems humanly possible. He has attended an untold number of plays, readings, lectures, baseball games, and even movie premieres to support his children and kvell. He has mentored young people and counseled family members through legal crises; he cared for his elderly and infirm mother until her death.

Sometimes I feel I am the only one who notices all this. Is it that these are things that fathers are supposed to do and so no one says anything about the amazing fact that they actually get done? Or maybe there is a medal I don't know about that is secretly awarded to men who give their entire lives so that their families and the rest of humankind will be better off. Really, I am serious. How come people aren't, like, blowing horns or organizing tributes to these guys? I don't get it.

It has taken me thirty-four years to understand the way my father loves. To understand that for him fathering is about self-sacrifice, or as one friend of mine says, "dying into one's children." When I was a small child, I missed my father when he went to his office, especially on weekends. As I grew older, I resented the fact that he disappeared into that netherland. As an adolescent I confronted him, accusing him of being a workaholic and trying to escape intimacy. Now, as a parent myself, I see more clearly his deep sense of responsibility, the integrity in his commitment to making sure his children started off with a solid foundation. He has put off so much of his own life for our development. I don't know that I agree with his choice, but I can't say I haven't benefited from it.

These days, my father comes from New York to visit me in San Francisco bearing gifts: a bag of my favorite chocolates and ten days of his time. He lets me sleep in the mornings and then picks me up in the big SUV I convince him to rent. We go to movies, walk around mountain lakes, and eat at all my favorite restaurants. We talk about all the books we plan to write, and all the cities in foreign lands we want to visit. We talk about the importance of fathers and the many, many men and women who don't have one. We talk about his first grandson, still swimming around in my belly. We talk about how much I will miss him when this life is over, and how much more this makes me appreciate him now.

JIMMY BUFFETT

Singer/songwriter/author with almost forty gold, platinum, and multiplatinum records and three No. 1 New York Times *best sellers; top-drawing concert attraction.*

MY FATHER TOOK ME TO see *The Spirit of St. Louis* when I was ten years old. He had been an aviator in World War II, flying as a crew chief on C-47s over the Burma hump. It was a strange undertaking for a man who came from a long line of sailors, and it wasn't until we were both much older that I learned why he had chosen to fly.

The images of Jimmy Stewart acting out the story of Charles Lindbergh got to both of us. By the third reel, my father and I were riding with Lucky Lindy in *The Spirit of St. Louis.* We were with him as he munched on his tuna sandwich, fought off fatigue, got lost, almost crashed into the ocean, and finally found the lights at Le Bourget airport in Paris. I still remember that day at the Loop Theater, in Mobile, when my dad and I jumped out of our seats and cheered as the wheels touched down. We sat and cried as Jimmy Stewart rode on the shoulders of the extras from central casting to the end of the movie. It was the first time I had ever seen my father cry.

Dad and I never really talked about his flying days. I was so enamored of the exploits of my grandfather that I forgot that my old man had had a few adventures of his own. My grandfather was at sea for months, sometimes years, at a time, and my dad became the father figure for his three younger siblings. When World War II broke out, my grandfather and my uncle both joined the navy. My father, however, joined the Army Air Corps, where he became a master sergeant. He was a flight mechanic and worked on B-17s in Maine, B-25s in Africa, and C-47s in India. After the war, he spent every day until he retired building ships and barges. Once I became romantically involved with airplanes, it became a wonderful opportunity to stay in touch with him. Until he died in 2003 he rode with me in every airplane I have owned, and there have been a lot of them.

In early 1995, he was diagnosed with Alzheimer's disease. My dad had been a whiz with facts and figures. He was a draftsman and a dynamo of energy with whom few people could keep pace. Now he had to face the awful reality that he was losing his mind. Once the devastating news settled in, our conversations were more personal than they had ever been. Dad had never been a talker, and when he did talk, it was about either his work at the shipyard or his children and grandchildren. Now he was scared and bewildered, and he said so. He never talked about licking Alzheimer's, as if it were some kind of opponent he was going to defeat. He knew his fate. He told me he just wanted to do a few things that he had never gotten to do. He was going to study his options and let me know how I could help.

One day I got a call from him, asking me to come to Alabama. I had no idea what my dad had come up with. He was mostly here in those days, but he could also go out into the cosmos. I didn't know if he would ask to go to Mars or mainland China. I started to flash on that old TV show *Run for Your Life*, starring Ben Gazzara. My father was not a big movie or television buff, but along with Jackie Gleason in *The Honeymooners* and James Arness in *Gunsmoke*, he loved Ben Gazzara in that series. Here's the basic plot: A wealthy and successful doctor finds out that he has only six months to live. The guy buys a fancy sports car and proceeds to travel around America, falling in love with beautiful women in exotic locations. I wondered if the old man was going to run for his life.

He met me at the airport and threw me the keys to the car. "You didn't like the way I drove even before I got this shit," he said. It was a small indication of his harsh reality, and his awareness that in desperate times and situations, humor is the only way out. We picked up a couple of oyster loaves and Barq's root beers at Mac's Cafe, then drove on to Homeport.

We were sitting at the end of the pier that my father had had built which ran from the house on the bluff for the length of four football fields. It was his signature upon the landscape of the eastern shore. As one of his neighbors had said upon its completion, "Goddamn, J.D., I guess you wanted them astronauts to see where you lived from outer space."

Flying around the roof were signal flags and flags from every country he had visited. Old Glory sat on the south corner on a solitary and lofty old mast. In the opposite corner stood his pride and joy, a barbecue pit and smoker fabricated in a sheet-metal shop out of materials left over from the refit of the aircraft carrier *Lexington*. It looked like a small nuclear reactor and weighed about as much. It had been dragged out of the shipyard under cloak of darkness and presented to him as a surprise from his coworkers upon his retirement. My dad called it his heirloom and the only material thing he really loved. He was going to leave it to me in his will—that is, as he said, "if you can move the son of a bitch."

We were looking out over the shallow waters of Mobile Bay, savoring the day and the taste of fresh fried oysters on buttered French bread with hot sauce and tartar sauce—the sandwich that's synonymous with the Gulf Coast. He drained the last of his Barq's and stared out across the bay. "You know what I was just thinking about?"

"What?" These days that could be a loaded question.

"Remember when you got thrown out of the sailing club for leaving the race and sailing all the way across the bay?" I only had to think a moment about that major event in my misspent youth. It had been the same kind of day as today.

"You bet I do," I said with a laugh.

"I never told you, but that was about as proud as I ever was of you. I mean, being the first Buffett to get a college degree was good, don't get me wrong, but that time you just decided to light out on your own, that was a moment."

Tears came into my eyes. I started to drift back to that incredible day, but my father's next words cut my trip short.

"I just saved you a hell of a lot of money," he said.

"What do you mean?" I asked, drying my eyes and swallowing hard.

"Well, I've decided where I want to go. I talked it over with your mom, and she thinks it's a good idea. I want to go to Salt Cay for Christmas."

"Salt Cay?" I said in disbelief. I was probably one of the very few people on the planet who had actually been to Salt Cay. It is a scruffy, parched little island to the south of Grand Turk in the Turks and Caicos Islands. Paris it ain't.

"This disease is strange, Jim. It takes you back, you know. When it hits, I can't remember shit about what I did two minutes ago, but I can see things in the past like I was there. I had some of the best times in my life on Salt Cay when your grandfather was loading salt bound for New Orleans. I was six years old, and we were on the *Chicamauga*. She lay at anchor, and I would go watch them load the salt and then I'd take off with a group of local kids, and we would chase flamingos and catch lobsters from the beach. I know, it ain't a place Ben Gazzara would go looking for his babes, but I want to go back."

He tossed some sticks to the dogs, who gallivanted into the shallow water to retrieve them. They swam back to the pier, shook the water from their fur, and dropped the sticks at our feet, waiting for the next toss. After several more throws, they sensed a change in mood and swam off toward the beach, leaving my father and me alone.

"It's getting worse, Jim," he said flatly. "It's the scariest thing I have ever been through in my life." I was in tears but couldn't speak. Saying I was sorry just didn't feel like enough. My dad sensed this immediately and changed the topic. "You know why I chose to fly instead of going to sea?"

There it was, the question that had been nagging at me all these years. Now, on the end of the pier near the end of his lucid days, I was going to get the answer. "Why?" I asked.

"Because it was what I wasn't supposed to do. Looks like you have made a career out of that, doing what you're not supposed to do. I'm proud of you, boy."

B. D. WONG

Tony Award–winning actor; series regular on Oz *and* Law & Order: Special Victims Unit; *director of the feature film* Social Grace; *author of* Following Foo: The Electronic Adventures of the Chestnut Man.

MY FOUR-YEAR-OLD SON LOVES THE New York subway system. What's not to love? It's loud. It's fast. It has practically the whole alphabet in it. Furthermore, taking the subway is truly an independent act. When I first took the subway by myself, I was finally a grown-up. I couldn't keep an apartment or a relationship, but I could get to the airport on the A train for a buck and a quarter, so as far as I was concerned I was grown up.

Once a week, my son and I go to a favorite spot in a major subway station, where we watch all four tracks of the Lexington Line pull in and out from a rare vantage point *above* all the action. I have always referred to the trains by color just to make things easier, but he refuses. It is never the *green* train; it is always the specific number that is actually *on* the train, and it is always either specifically an express or a local, depending on which track it squeals in on. On those inevitable occasions when the MTA changes things around a little to keep weekend straphangers on their toes, he has been known to say things like, "The 6 train is on the express track, Dad. *Why? Do you believe it?*"

For the past year we have been doing this together. I bet in every parent/child relationship there is a delicious intimacy in those tiny rituals that only you share with your offspring. My father took me to the ballet several times during my childhood, and it was "our thing." Our son's other Daddy and he share a daily morning bike ride, followed by a muffin or bagel in the courtyard between two high-rises, weather permitting. Daddy and Dad share a great relish in our son's growing ability to enjoy a simple conversation about any random thing.

Early this year I would pick him up and push him in his stroller to our spot (which he pointedly refers to as *your favorite spot*, which makes me sometimes wonder if he is simply tolerating all of this to entertain *me*). At a little more than three, he petered out easily when walking on his own, so I dutifully pushed him in the toddler SUV. Today, independence is encouraged. We have phased out the stroller completely, so now we go to *my favorite spot* sans stroller, hand in hand, chatting, or negotiating about whether or not I will carry him. Just for the heck of it, we take the humid elevators that lift us from the train platform to the station level, and up to the street. Development is a mixed bag for me. I am proud of his progress, yet nostalgic for the strollers and baby bottles and baby talk. Besides, elevators are big machines that you can get inside and they move and make motor sounds and *ding* and they have buttons in them and you meet the most interesting New Yorkers in them who always tell you how cute you are. So we eschew independence once in a while for the proverbial free ride. One day soon, I know, the elevator will be added to the growing list of things from the Good Old Days.

Speaking of the Good Old Days, my own father is in town this week with my mom, to visit me at work and to see their youngest grandson. My brothers and I are uncannily like each of my parents in a lot of ways. It's my emotional personality that I find to be one of my most vital blood vessels leading from my heart directly to my father's. When making *meaningful* statements, my voice always chokes in exactly the same way I've heard from him for so many years. It's always surprising to me how deep these family traits run; how the furrows in my life path are so intensely lichened with the vivid DNA of my ancestors. Was my great-great-grandfather like this, too?

I decided to take my dad to one of *our* favorite spots, a little Chinese-owned massage joint in the Village. Visiting New York ain't that easy for my dad. He's in his eighties and kind of asthmatic, so we mostly just cab around, or as on the last few visits, I rent a wheelchair and just push him everywhere.

This time, my folks happen to be visiting during the Republican National Convention. Which is a trip, because New York just doesn't quite know what to do with itself this week. Getting a cab is not easy. There are a lotta guys in cowboy hats and ladies with big hair getting in front of you. My apartment is near a subway station, though, and the massage place is near a station, so I figured we could grab the train, and, as with our son, I decided to forgo pushing him for the glorious independence of walking. My mom decided to go shopping while Dad and I got "pummeled."

At the stairs going down to the station, we made a plan to reconnoiter with Mom. Then my dad had a pretty customary fit of sentimentality, manifested in a completely noncustomary fashion. As Mom tottered off her way and we went ours, Dad called, "I love you" to her, as if she were about to be swallowed up by the Scylla and Charybdis of descending Republicana and he might never see her again. It was at once amusing and moving.

The route to the massage joint is the same one I have taken my son on maybe a hundred times this year.

Well, something memorable happened when my dad touched the handrail to go down the stairs. As I told him, "Hold the rail," I heard myself speaking in the exact same voice, in the exact same rhythm and cadence, that I've used to coach my own son down the exact same stairs more than a hundred times as he went down with the same halting, hesitating dependence on that rail.

When we got downstairs, I showed him, ever so patiently, how to swipe a MetroCard at the turnstile. It took several tries, but eventually the mechanism made that familiar sound condoning his approach, and he pushed through the turnstile with the same satisfaction, and the same newness, and the same expression of *"Like that?"* that his grandson showed me on his first swipe not too many weekends ago.

There was one transfer point in the ride, at the same hub station where *my favorite spot* is. As we passed it, I mentioned, like a tour guide, "This is where your grandson and I watch the trains every week. It's our favorite spot." Like clockwork, my throat clenched and I got all gooey and weepy inside, and then I quickly evened out my line-reading, lest I reveal the sap hidden within me.

To make things easier on the old guy, I guided him to all the various elevators that go from train to mezzanine and back down to another train, only I didn't offer that he could push the buttons. As with my other beloved subway companion, I just enjoyed this rare time alone with him, and I got a little misty remembering those days when he could climb up on the roof to get a lost ball or throw me up onto his shoulders at the beach. We had a couple of world-class back rubs, and reversed our travel itinerary, meeting my mom in time for dinner, as she had thankfully not been abducted by rednecks.

I am not afraid of death. I am not really afraid of my own death, and as long as I don't live foolishly I don't believe I can do anything much about anyone else's, I really don't. I daresay our son, born woefully premature, faked Death out in his first four months more times than most people do in a lifetime, and I am grateful for this on a daily basis. But what next? Will he live long enough to "make his parents (even more) proud"? Let's talk turkey. I have no idea.

As life continues to unroll its cozy green sleeping bag, and night after night I climb into the flannel lining decorated with the hunters and the ducks, I find myself beat from working my ass off daily. I suppose, when I really think about it, the main reason for this is to make my folks, and my son, proud of me, maybe now more than ever. Since my son came into my psyche-delic theatrical universe, I have looked at life, and death, very differently. Fatherhood was a one-way street before he came to the party. Now that he's here, I can appreciate it as a father and as a son simultaneously.

Let's talk turkey. Who knows what tomorrow will bring? I know why my dad blurts out "I love you" to his wife of more than fifty years as she embarks on a simple errand in the Big Apple. He does it because the great thing, and the terrible thing, *and the great thing,* about life is that you never know. You never know.

One thing I am pretty sure I do know, however, is that my folks are proud of me, and my brothers, and all of our children. Even though I'm busting my butt to make it big in New York City, I know it doesn't matter. He is a proud and happy and content man. If he lives to the age of his own mother, we all get more than ten years with him. My son would be a teenager. That would be amazing. But, gobble-gobble. You never know.

Every day I think about this, and every day I realize that I simply cannot fully comprehend all of the things my dad (and mom) went through to raise me and my brothers, to make ends meet, to deal with the incredible stresses and strains, to instill humane values in us, and I am humbled and awestruck. So, of course, I realize it is I who should be proud of *him.* I am a bit ashamed to admit that it took having a son of my own, but I guess that's life.

Let's talk turkey. I understand now, Dad.

NINA TOTENBERG

*National Public Radio's award-winning
legal-affairs correspondent and a frequent
contributor to major newspapers and periodicals.*

WHEN I WAS GROWING UP, people would often ask me if
I was violinist Roman Totenberg's daughter. I was always thrilled to say, "I am," for Roman Totenberg was—and
is—a remarkable musician, father, and human being.

His life has been an incredible odyssey. A child prodigy before he was ten, he traveled from the famines of Eastern Europe
to the palaces of Old Europe, and eventually to the White House
of his adopted country, the United States.

As I write this, my father, who will, God willing, be ninety-
four when this is published, is in Poland giving master classes,
teaching, and playing at a music festival, where he is being appro-
priately feted by adoring students and faculty. When he returns,
he will be back teaching at Boston University. Indeed, I doubt
there is a major orchestra in the world today that is without a

violinist trained by Roman Totenberg, and many of the soloists who transfix audiences worldwide were his students, too. Long after they have left his tutelage, students write to him, seeking advice about their lives, their marriages, their children, and, of course, their careers. He never fails to help, to advise, to gently pat on the back, or raise an eyebrow, or offer help. To see how he cares for his students is to know the meaning of the word *mentor*.

Often they come from different countries and cultures, and he never fails to help them find their way professionally and personally, whether it is finding a place for them to live or a new approach to a difficult concerto. Not that he isn't paid back many times over. They dote on him. With my mother now gone from this earth, I often call home to find a covey of young people making dinner for the "Maestro."

My father learned to play the violin almost by accident when he was five. His father, an architect, was in Moscow on some sort of project. With both parents working during the day, and no one to take care of little Roman, the guy who lived in the apartment upstairs agreed to babysit. The man was at home during the day because he was the concertmaster of the Moscow Philharmonic. At a loss over what to do with a five-year-old, he taught him to play the violin. Within months, the teacher and the boy were playing concerts together. And five years later, my father made his debut as a soloist with the Warsaw Philharmonic. It was the beginning of a grand concert career that has lasted for eight decades.

That last sentence makes it somehow sound easy. But it

wasn't. In the early part of the twentieth century, when famines ravaged Poland and Russia, there were times when little Roman was literally the breadwinner. Unlike his father, he was not paid with money but with food, and there was no food to eat anywhere. He remembers that when a horse would fall in the street, it would be set upon by the crowds and within moments dismembered for food.

As he won prizes and plaudits throughout Europe, he saw a life he had never imagined. As a young man, he played a concert for the king of Italy. It was an extremely formal event—so formal that he had to borrow the required black cape and top hat from the Polish ambassador. And when he finished performing, he had to back out of the room so that his back was never to the king.

Shortly thereafter, he came on his first trip to the United States and made a huge splash, with rave reviews. He was invited to the White House to perform, and he recalls running around the White House trying to find a place to change, and then afterwards being entertained by President Roosevelt in the family quarters, where Mrs. Roosevelt personally served the performers their dinner. He remembers what a contrast it was to the formality and rigidity of the Italian scene, and he remembers saying to himself, "This is the country for me!"

What has he taught my two sisters and me? Just the important things: decency, courage, the value of hard work, love of family, and, of course, to always maintain a sense of humor.

To see your father standing in front of a great symphony orchestra or on the recital stage of Carnegie Hall, and to hear this miraculous music emanating from his violin and his heart, is to know how many times he practiced each passage, how no day passed, ever, without hours of practicing. Nothing is effortless even if it looks as though it is. And so when I sweat over a sentence for one of my stories, or I make that seventy-fifth phone call, or read another boring brief, I know that nothing that seems effortless really is.

I think of him when I learn something new, or try a new way of doing a task. After all, he is ninety-four, and he's still learning new pieces. It is interesting for him, a challenge. Two years ago he played a long recital in Boston, and he learned some new material, difficult material, for the performance. That is no small task. When you are over ninety, the fingers don't learn as easily. And yes, the pieces he played flawlessly in that concert, from Brahms to Paganini, were the ones he had played for decades. The new ones, while less perfect, were still incredibly beautiful. Indeed, my father is so devoted to change and progress that when he heard me playing one of his recordings of the Bach solo sonatas, recordings that he made some thirty years ago, he remarked, "I play those very differently now. I've decided Bach wanted to do something entirely different."

I credit my father with my having a career at all. I grew up at a time when there were no women in news. None. So what gave me the idea I could do this? Well, there were women performers in music. My father considered them equals. They were equals. And he always seemed to expect that his daughters could do anything they wished. I'm not sure he had any idea what the news world was like. He just assumed that if I worked hard and was good at what I did, I would succeed.

He is an incredibly sweet person but with an inner toughness, and I expect he taught me that, too. I suppose people always thought I was a tough reporter, but I knew that at heart I was mush. When my late husband suffered a major head injury, I was in despair and really wondered if I could take care of him in the way he deserved. My father and my mother never seemed to have any doubts that I would—and I did for five years.

My father taught me to stand for something, too. He is a person who, very gently, will not be pushed around. Even if it costs him, and it has on occasion, he follows the path he thinks is right. During the Anita Hill episode, a time that was, for me, something of a personal trial, I didn't talk to him at all for weeks. I was wildly busy. And one day, out of nowhere, when it was completely over, he said to me on the phone, "You know, Ninotchka, I'm very proud of you." It gave me goose bumps.

My father teases me now that people ask him, "Are you Nina Totenberg's father?" And he's thrilled to say, "I am."

MATT LAUER

Co-anchor, the Today *show.*

WHEN I WAS A KID, my dad was a bicycle salesman and he had the northeast as his territory. He used to travel a lot, and my earliest recollections are of him putting me in the car and driving to places like New Hampshire, Boston, and Vermont. We would visit bike stores and stay in little roadside motels. The most vivid early memory is one I talked about until the day he died—stopping in some roadside diner in New Hampshire and having a hamburger and a piece of apple pie. That apple pie grew in stature so by the end of his life, it was the best piece of apple pie ever created by any human being.

I also remember my father at Little League games. Those were very important times for me, but my parents divorced when I was eight, so the memories after that became different. It was weekends with my dad and weekdays with my mom.

You hear so much about children of divorce. Either I was naive and just not paying attention, or my parents did it as well as any two parents have ever done it. I never felt animosity. My dad and mom decided at some point they couldn't be married anymore but they still liked each other as people. When my father came to pick us up on weekends, it wasn't one of those situations you hear about where the dad sits in the driveway and honks the horn, waiting for the mother who pushes the kids out the door after saying something nasty about the father. He would come in, have a drink. If there were no urgent plans he would have dinner.

When there were big occasions like graduations, birthdays, or Christmas, we would often do them together—my mom and my dad, and his new wife and her new husband, the stepfamilies as well. They did it so well that for me it was going from having two great parents to having four great parents. It was a bonus.

My father loved the game of golf. His father had taught him how to play, and he was one of these guys who had a naturally good swing. He didn't have to work at it much, and he could shoot in the 80s whether he played twice a week or twice a year. He had a natural ability. He taught me to play by the time I was ten, and there is no doubt in my mind that that's one of the reasons I love golf so much. After my parents' divorce, I'd go to my dad's craving time with him and while learning, we would spend four or five hours of solid time together on a golf course. Regardless of how I played, it was quality time with a capital Q.

I'm sure that's one of the main reasons the game has such an allure for me—it triggers wonderfully warm memories of our time together.

The one conscious thought I had about being a father myself and relating it to how my dad was as a father was that my dad's greatest quality was reliability. I don't mean that in a boring sense. He was a man of great character and you could count on his reasoning, on his moral compass. You could count on the fact that he was with you win, lose, or tie, and so when I'm dealing with my children I think the one thing I want them to remember about me is that no matter what, they can count on me. At this age to protect them, to make them laugh, to comfort them. As they get older, to come to when they have problems, when they have done something right or something wrong. This was really the greatest gift my father gave me.

The most noticeable change in me since I became a parent is that I've loosened up. I sing Elmo songs at the top of my lungs as I'm driving down the highway. When I'm with my son in a crowd of people and the Wiggles are in front of us, I'm much more willing to do the Wiggles dance. I didn't know I would be capable of that kind of thing.

My priorities have changed, too. Before I had a child, I was driven by work, especially this job at the *Today* show. Until I got married, it was the most important thing in my life. And when I got married, it took on co-equal status because there was so much that had to go on in the early days. Now it's a distant third. I don't experience the highs I used to with work, but it's nice because I don't experience the lows, either. I used to define myself by what happened in my career. I now define myself by what happens when I walk into the apartment at night.

Maybe it's different for other people, but for me being a parent is so far beyond what I imagined that it's hard to believe. It used to be that I'd get done with a busy workweek, and I would have to figure out things to do so that the weekend would be great. I wanted to go out to dinner with friends; I wanted to play golf. Now a weekend spent at the house where we have zero plans and may never leave the driveway is what's great. I spend two or three hours on the floor with Jack or Romey building a little train set, teaching them how to swim in the pool, playing tag, putting them on the slide, and talking with them.

Once a week, rain or shine, I have lunch with Jack, just the two of us. Usually I take him downstairs to the Rock Center Café. I am never in a better mood than after I have talked to him for an hour. Conversations are all over the place and sometimes they don't make a lot of sense, but an hour of conversing with him is the best part of my week.

I've started to take Jack out to play golf with me. I put him in the cart and he hits the ball a couple of times and we ride up the fairways. There's a wonderful picture I have of my dad with his father, sitting on a golf course with clubs in his hand. I've got lots of pictures of my dad and me on the golf course.

I would love to have one of my dad, me, and Jack on the golf course. The fact that my dad never got to know Jack or

Romey—worse, that they never got to meet my dad, their grand-father—is probably the only bittersweet aspect.

I was thirty-seven when my dad died and I never had a doubt in my thirty-seven years that no matter what happened, my dad would be there without questions asked. Whether I was unem-ployed and needing emotional guidance, whether I was going through a divorce and needing emotional guidance, whether I was needing financial support. I never had to hesitate and I knew I wouldn't get a lecture; I knew it wouldn't be used as a life les-son; I knew it wouldn't be rubbed in my face. I just knew he would be there for me when I went to him. I hope that I will be thought of by my children in that same way.

BONNIE RAITT

Nine-time Grammy Award–winning singer-songwriter, with seventeen albums, including Bonnie Raitt *(1971),* Nick of Time *(1989),* Luck of the Draw *(1991), and* The Best of Bonnie Raitt on Capitol 1989–2003.

M Y DAD, JOHN RAITT, HAS played more roles as a leading man than anybody in Broadway history. He was the original Billy Bigelow in *Carousel* and Sid Sorokin in *The Pajama Game,* then he did twenty-five consecutive years of summer stock, starring in *Carousel, Oklahoma!, The Pajama Game, The Music Man, Annie Get Your Gun, Kiss Me Kate, Camelot, Man of La Mancha,* as well as starring in the national touring companies of *Zorba* and *Shenandoah.* We moved to California when he made the movie of *Pajama Game* in 1957.

My mother, Marjory, was a wonderful pianist and my dad's accompanist and music director. They would rehearse for his concerts and shows all the time, and it really helped make my two brothers and me so musical, having this incredible heritage right there in our home. We would see my dad perform when we took a week off from camp and got to join him on the road. Years later, my dad couldn't believe I knew the lyrics to so many Broadway shows. He asked, "Where in the world did you learn all that?" I said, "Dad, all those years you did summer stock, I sat in the wings and learned every line."

I saw as a kid that my dad gave everything he had in every performance. Where most stars in his position would be concerned about when they'd get their next shot at Broadway, it never seemed to matter much to him. He really loved taking the classics out to where the people are—to the wonderful network of regional theaters filled with fans who might not ever get to New York but would faithfully come out every year to experience the magic that is live theater. To this day, so many of my fans come up and tell me how thrilled they were to get to see my dad in one of those shows and what an incredible performance he gave.

To my dad, every night is opening night—every show as important as any other. I saw the commitment he made to honoring both the material and his audience year in and year out. This made a huge impression on me.

He lives very much in the moment. He has an innate ability to pick himself up from any setback or loss and just, as he says, "move on down the road." This deliberate focus is, I think, a big part of the reason he's continued to stay in such strong voice, such good physical and mental health, all these years, and surely why he seems much happier and less neurotic than most stars you tend to find in the dodgy and mercurial world of show business. It took me some time to get the healthy lifestyle right, but I certainly admire these lessons of making every day and show count, of respecting the gift that is our talent and this amazing job we get to do for a living.

I came into my music through folk music, though, not my dad's tradition. I got my first guitar when I was eight, after picking up an interest in folk songs at camp from the college kids who were our counselors, leading songs around the fire. The folk craze was hitting all the colleges—almost every campus was rife with intense Ian & Sylvia, Joan Baez, and Bob Dylan types; Peter, Paul and Mary and the Kingston Trio had big hits on the radio. Along with Motown and the Beatles, this was really the music of my time. I begged for a guitar for Christmas, but for a long time it was just a hobby for me. I didn't distinguish between singing my dad's songs or Joan Baez, blues, or Beatles tunes; I liked them all.

As a performer, I do ballads mixed in with rock 'n' roll, blues, and all kinds of songs, but I never thought I'd be able to sing my dad's music. Sometime around the Grammys and the success of *Nick of Time*, the Boston Pops called and invited my dad and me to sing together for a PBS special. He'd been coming onstage at the end of my shows for years, rousing the audience up on their feet to join him in singing "Oklahoma!" My trying his songs was another matter, especially backed by an orchestra. After wondering how it could possibly work, I realized I'd learned to sing ballads from him in the first place. He would tell me, "It's all telling a story—a great song is a great song, whether it's 'Angel from Montgomery' or 'If I Loved You.' "

We'd been singing show tunes in the pool together for years, grabbing some precious dad/daughter time, swimming with our heads above water and seeing how many songs we could remember. I came down off the I-gotta-be-a-bad-blues-mamma platform I think I was on for the first twenty years of my career and realized at forty that there were beautiful songs we could do together. The Pops show was a wonderful success, and we've gone on to sing with each other on many tours and shows since. In 1995 we had the chance to record together on his album *Broadway Legend*. We sang "Hey There" and "Anything You Can Do" and my favorite, "They Say It's Wonderful." Singing with him has been one of my life's greatest gifts.

He's been a great dad because he's been very nonjudgmental. He accepts the rock 'n' roll part of what I do, and he accepted the lifestyle that goes with it. He never came down on me for any of my choices. He would just gently say, "If you take care of yourself, your voice will stay," that kind of thing. He let us kids grow in our own unique way and time, always letting us know he'd be there for us, and that's a wonderful gift to have from a dad. He's also been, along with my mother, a real inspiration for my social activism. He set us on the road to believing we should give something back, working for issues like peace and justice, standing up for what we believe. He leads by example and not by censoring.

And what a gift to be able to go into your dad's line of work—both my folks' line of work—with all the joy and excitement of getting paid to do something you love so much. And then to have gotten the career recognition I did with him there with me, and my mom at home watching, that night in 1990 when I won all those Grammys. When I came back to my seat, he stood up to give me a hug, then he started to lose it. And then so did I. They cut to a commercial, but the whole Shrine Auditorium could see us just holding on to each other, our shoulders shaking for a long time.

Most big guys like him, they don't cry much. And being raised Scotch-Presbyterian, he learned to squelch a lot of those strong feelings. He sure doesn't onstage, but in real life he isn't a big-emoting kind of guy. It was very powerful and very, very moving. It was an incredible thing to make him so proud.

DANIEL HANDLER
(AKA LEMONY SNICKET)

Author of The Basic Eight, Watch Your Mouth, *and the forthcoming* Adverbs, *and (allegedly) twelve books under the name Lemony Snicket.*

M Y FATHER, LOUIS HANDLER, HAS a group of friends that he's been playing bridge with every week since before I was born, and I'm thirty-four. Some of them have recently passed on, so there are some new members, but there was a core club for twenty or twenty-five years. They watched each other become fathers and grandfathers over the bridge table. They would meet at each other's houses—we lived near the West Portal neighborhood of San Francisco—so about once a month there would be four guys in my living room playing bridge on Tuesday night. When I was little, I would go to sleep to the sound of them arguing over individual hands. They played a penny a point, and on Wednesday morning there might be a small pile of money on the kitchen counter that my father had won; it would often be as high as $2.50. Or there might be nothing, and occasionally I would go into the living room and beg my father in the style of the old melodramas not to spend the children's insulin money on bridge. (Being a humorist was required of everyone in my family.)

My father is a great talker. He's good at explaining the world. So when he first tried to teach me how to play bridge, he made the game pretty clear. We sat in the breakfast room, at the table where we ate all our meals except when there was company, and we probably each had a glass of seltzer in front of us. I must have been in second or third grade. I was sort of resistant to it then, but I think after adolescence, many people come back to their fathers and say, "It looks like you were right after all." I saw that there was quite a bit of worth in learning to play a game that seemed a form of cultural literacy, universally recognized as a way to sit with one's friends without spending much money and having a sort of hook to hang conversation on.

Bridge was an example of masculinity that was intelligent and genteel, and that was very appealing to me. I was never somebody to sit in a stadium or go out and play football, and neither was my father. This was something that also seemed a particularly male activity. Not exclusively, of course; whenever we went on a family vacation, my parents would find other people to play with. But it seemed a way, for men especially, to hang out together that wasn't barbarian. I saw the camaraderie of my dad and his friends, a lot of laughter and conversation as they played this game that is sort of cerebral and certainly not physically taxing, and that's a model of masculinity you don't see a lot. It's certainly a model of masculinity I hope to present to my infant son, Otto. Of course, it's about the only one I can present to him.

And there are all sorts of life metaphors you can derive from bridge. You require a good partner, and you need to learn to communicate in a way that is clear to some people and obscure to others. You need to know when you're in a position of power and when you're in a position of weakness; and there's an aspect of bridge called the finesse—where you're sort of tricking the opposition into using their firepower on a less worthy target so that they have no firepower left over, meaning that you're getting people to give things up that they wouldn't ordinarily; that's very important in life—and you need a bit of luck.

It's been a constant in my life. I played bridge with my father before I left home; then when I was in college, I started to play with more seriousness, and I would call him and ask him for strategic tips. Later, I taught my wife, Lisa Brown, to play. We were living in Manhattan, we were broke, and we wanted to socialize without spending one hundred dollars, which is pretty difficult in Manhattan. So we would invite people over. We had a sort of vintage-cocktail dictionary, and each week we would make some odd cocktail and play bridge. I still called my father for strategic advice, and we'd play bridge whenever he visited. Now we all live in San Francisco again, and we all still play. Thanks to my father I've never been starved for cheap amusement.

CONAN O'BRIEN

■

Talk show host; male model; mini–sub enthusiast.

I'M ONE OF SIX CHILDREN, and when you travel in a pack like that, your early memories of your father all involve discipline. For the longest time, my dad was simply a black-haired arm reaching into the backseat trying to grab one of us. It always reminded me of the famous scene in *King Kong* where the hero is trapped on the cliff face while Kong is blindly reaching around, trying to crush him with his giant fist. My father believed in frontier justice. He'd say, "I don't know who broke the clock in the front hall, so you're all going to be punished." It seemed unfair at the time, but now that it has become the basis for our country's foreign policy, I'm starting to think my father was on to something.

Kids connect first with their mother, so for the longest time in early childhood your dad is an abstraction. All of us knew that my father was a doctor and that he went off to something called a lab, but none of us had any concept what that really meant. He may as well have been a riverboat gambler because none of us understood anything about the science of battling infectious disease. To be honest, I still can't quite explain to people what my dad does for a living so I often just say that he's a cardsharp on a steamboat called *The Mississippi Belle*.

Though I'm very proud of my dad's work battling infectious disease, it's not easy being the child of a doctor. When a child wants to skip school for a day so he can drink ginger ale and watch *The Price Is Right,* the most common excuse is "I've got a sore throat." Unfortunately, in our house a sore throat was cause for immediate scientific exploration. The second I said my throat hurt my dad would take me into his study to take a culture of the back of my throat. And, by his own admission, my father is not talented at taking a throat culture. He'd pull out a foot-long swab with a cotton tip and jam it down my throat, looking for suspicious microbes. It's supposed to be a quick procedure, but my father would have that stick down my throat for half an hour, rooting around as if he were a tired plumber snaking a toilet. By the time my dad was done, I really did have a sore throat.

As time went on and I grew older, I came to appreciate my dad's sense of humor. My father is a very funny guy with a great feel for visual comedy. He'd often take us to revival houses to see Charlie Chaplin, the Marx Brothers, or W. C. Fields. He also loved the *Pink Panther* films and made sure that we saw all of them, and I think it was watching those films with my father that initially sparked my interest in being a comedian. I was also very aware as a child that my father was usually the funny person in the room. I saw the way he could make other adults at a party laugh and that was my first exposure to the power of being funny. It was also where I learned the power of making sure that people around you have had plenty to drink. To this day, I always make sure that my audience is three sheets to the wind before I tell a joke.

Much later, when I started to write and perform comedy in college, my dad was very supportive. Many people have assumed that because my father is a research scientist and a medical professor that he would discourage a career in television, but on the contrary, he has always encouraged me. I have a theory that any anxiety your parents may have about your career evaporates the minute you can pay your own rent. I sometimes think that if I had called my dad after moving to Los Angeles in 1985 and said, "I'm strangling railroad tramps and stealing their cash," he'd have said, "Well, as long as you're working."

The truth, though, is that my dad has always gone out of his way to tell me when something I do makes him laugh. Sometimes, he'll even go on to tell me, very specifically, *why* it was funny. Occasionally during these explanations I get very confused and forget what we're talking about, but it's nice to know the man cares.

As for me, I didn't get married until after my career was up and running. I think when you come from a large family you spend so much time trying to establish your own identity that when you're finally out in the world and on your own, you're not in a hurry to team up. At least that's my excuse for not getting a date for fifteen years. I married when I was thirty-eight, and by then I was ready to have kids right away. I felt strongly that I didn't want to be an old dad. I had this vision of me as Mr. Burns on *The Simpsons* watching my children play through the glass window on my hyperbaric oxygen-chamber. "Smithers—massage my heart back to life, then go tell my children I love them." Even though very few people in my family are blessed with real athletic ability, it's important to me that I be a young enough dad to be able to toss a ball around with my kid. And by *ball* I mean one of those huge Nerf-things. God forbid I toss a real ball and get hurt.

Fatherhood for me started when my daughter, Neve, was born a year ago. Even though it has been a while, I still can't tell you what it's like to become a father because, thirteen months later, the shock has not worn off. Immediately after the birth the doctor handed me some scissors and told me to cut the umbilical cord. First of all, this seemed like a union violation to me, and second, it seemed like an odd time to start someone off on surgical training. But we men are task-oriented, so it was probably the doctor's way of keeping me from passing out. At that moment he could easily have told me to tighten the distributor cap on a Dodge Caravan and I would have done it.

It takes time, after you become a dad, to assess what has really happened to you. When they hand you that baby for the first time it's as if they give you a giant shot of novocaine right in the forehead. Instantly I was transformed into this big, dumb, happy guy who has trouble articulating complex thoughts. My first moment of really feeling anything like a father was when they took Neve in for a hearing test the day after she was born. It's a standard test, but for some reason the technician had trouble getting a reading on one of my daughter's eardrums. It turned out that everything was fine, but for three minutes I had this overpowering fear that something might be wrong. And that's when I had my first clue as to how it feels to be a parent. Parenting is mindless fear, senseless rage, and a pair of torn slippers from the Truman administration.

And now I get to see my daughter with my father, which is hilarious. My father has morphed into this kindly, patient, fun-loving grandfather with no trace of a temper. The only time he's going to be reaching into the backseat to get at Neve is to hand her a chocolate bunny. It's completely unfair. Someday my dad will be taking Neve off to see the circus and I'll be shouting after her, "You don't get it, kid, in 1974 this guy was Stalin!"

Of course, many people say that grandparents get all the fun of parenting with none of the responsibility, but I have my own theory. It has been scientifically proven that testosterone levels in men start falling in their late twenties, so the authoritarian enforcer we know as kids mellows over time and becomes the kindly, doting grandfather. I'm already a much kinder, relaxed dad today than I would have been in my twenties. Of course, my testosterone levels started falling when I was eleven, so by the time my daughter is in college I'll technically be her grandmother. Won't that be nice. . . .

KATIE COURIC

Co-anchor, the Today *show.*

WHENEVER I WANT TO KNOW the answer to a question, I can look it up, or I can call my dad. I think it was in my genes to become a journalist because my dad—and my mom, but especially my dad—has an unbelievable natural curiosity. He is a voracious reader, and he can talk fluently on almost any subject, whether it's ancient history or a certain book or a geopolitical situation somewhere in the world. He's amazing in that way. I get my love of words and writing ability from him.

He thought journalism would be a good field for me because of my outgoing personality, and because I worked well under pressure. He used to laugh seeing me do my homework in front of the front door as I waited for the school bus, because I was such a procrastinator. His favorite word for me was *irrepressible.* My mother would be laughing at me at the dinner table, and my dad would be trying not to laugh as he said to her, "Elinor, please don't encourage her." And yet I knew he was getting a kick out of my silliness as well. He would try to talk about certain things, and I would start snoring, and he would get exasperated because we were making fun of him, but he always encouraged us.

My parents raised four responsible, accomplished children, and they were always present in our lives. They were very involved, but not to the point where it felt stifling. They had just the right amount of ambition for us: wanting to see us succeed and do our best. When any of us ran for school office—and we all did, with varying degrees of success—my dad would help write our speeches and my mom would help do our posters. Everything was a concerted effort in our family. We always ate together. We brought new words to the table.

I grew up in a comfortable but not opulent household. We didn't take a lot of fancy vacations or belong to the country club. My parents taught us values such as putting away money for college and gave us opportunities such as piano lessons and sports. And they let us be kids. Education was an important thing for both my parents, but we had a lot of free time—I could spend all day on my bicycle or playing ball in the street. I wish I knew what it was that made us the people we are today and gave us all such a strong sense of ourselves. I guess the biggest thing was love, matched with discipline, with high expectations but not so high that we could never reach them. There weren't so many expectations that we felt stressed-out.

My parents have been happily married for sixty years now, and I know that when I married Jay, I saw a lot of my dad in him: someone who was kind, highly intelligent, sophisticated, and fluent in a lot of subjects. Jay had a great love of history, as does my dad, and he loved the fact that I have many ancestors who fought in the Civil War and have deep roots in the South.

One of my most moving memories of my dad is when he came to the hospital once when Jay had to have complicated surgery having to do with his cancer. It was a hellacious time, and I was, needless to say, a basket case. I walked into New York Hospital and saw my dad waiting for me. He hadn't told me he was coming, and to see him, with his big set of white hair and looking so elegant in his suit—to have him there with me made me feel so much better. My parents are the kind of people who put their children above everything, and I feel so blessed that they are still with me. They are both responsible for the person I am. It's because of them that I have the strength to deal with some of the challenges I've had to face.

Since my dad is such a strong father figure for me, he can give me the perspective of a father when it comes to my daughters, Ellie and Carrie. When he visited recently and we went out to dinner, he noticed that Ellie asked if she could taste the wine I was drinking. Obviously, she's coming to the age where she's going to have a lot of peer pressure. I tried not to make a big deal of it and let her have a little taste, and later my dad said to me, "Have you sat down and talked to Ellie about drinking and alcohol?" I said, "Not that much." And he said, "I want you to talk to her about respecting alcohol; about how it can impair your judgment and make you do things you don't want to do— how you can't abuse it and have to wait until you're responsible in order to enjoy it."

I thought my dad was so wise to mention it. He is very careful not to inject himself too much. He's more of a quiet presence, but I think he is extraordinarily attuned to some of the things you need to do when you're raising a child. I feel I can talk to my dad about anything from politics to television to what's happening in the world to child-care issues. I don't know when it changed, but I certainly feel that he's not only my father but also a very close friend. Jay and I used to laugh and say that when it came to double-dating, we'd rather go out with my parents than with anybody else. It's a nice thing to be able to say.

I used to call my dad every day after the show; I still call him to find out what he thought about certain interviews. One time I interviewed David Duke, the white supremacist and former head of the Ku Klux Klan, and I was very hostile to him because of his views; some of the things he had said were so repugnant to any fair-minded person. When I called my dad after that show, he told me, "Edward R. Murrow said, 'Sometimes you have to take a stand; that's your moral obligation.' You did the right thing by giving David Duke such a hard time." My dad has continued to be my barometer in terms of what I do on the show and my desire to be fair yet challenging to everyone. His input and guidance have been invaluable.

Television is such a showy profession. Some parents might brag, but mine don't believe in bragging about any of their children. There is nothing that turns them off more. They are very proud of what I do, but I remember one time my dad was at the garage getting his car fixed, and someone asked him, "Are you Katie Couric's father?" He said, "No, she's my daughter."

MARY ROACH

■

Author of the New York Times *best seller* Stiff: The
Curious Lives of Human Cadavers *(W.W. Nor-
ton), whose work has appeared in* GQ, The New
York Times Magazine, Discover, Outside, Wired,
Salon, The Believer, *and many other publications.*

FOR SOMEONE WHO MADE HIS LIVING as a professor, my
father, Wally Roach, was not big on lessons. Having escaped a childhood of lower-class squalor in the industrial mid-
lands of England and remade himself into a dapper, well-spoken
PhD in New Hampshire, he would from time to time impart
some random nugget of upper-crust etiquette. *When eating soup,
always move the spoon away from you.* At a party not long after
I graduated from college, I heard a woman tell a moving story
about the time her father sat her down and taught her the importance of honesty. I tried to think of something similarly profound
that my father had taught me. Pathetically, the soup came to
mind. And a memory from my alphabet years: sitting on Pop's lap
in our old silver Chevy, me going "C-H-E-V," whereupon he'd
say "R-O," and I'd finish off the exchange: "L-E-T." Then we'd
switch parts.

"My father taught me how to spell Chevrolet," I said, and then excused myself to get a martini, which, my father had taught me, is best taken very dry and with two olives.

The exchange shook me. Was it possible I had learned nothing from the man who had raised me? I tried to think of a time when I'd turned to Pop for answers. All I came up with was being about six years old and asking my father what LBJ stood for. Here was my father's chance to introduce his daughter to the basics of American government. He said, "Lollipops, buttercups, and jelly beans."

Because my father was English, because he was sixty-five years older than I, because he was a better storyteller than listener, we didn't do a lot of heart-to-heart talking. I think that if it were possible to be part of a family and never actually talk about anything serious, my dad would have done so. Whatever he taught me, I guess he taught me by example. Shortly after the party incident, I got out a pad and wrote down the images and memories of my father that first came to mind. It didn't look good. Right away, I remembered the time he drove me and my neighbor Becky the three miles to the Etna general store on the hood of the car (by now a Plymouth), going what felt like fifty mph but was probably twenty, the two of us squealing with joy the whole way. I recalled him hitchhiking to the store if my brother had the car. When I was twelve, he painted a life-sized elephant on the basement floor because that was my favorite animal. I remembered him drawing caricatures of strangers—fellow diners at the Valley's Steakhouse—on the backs of our placemats. I pictured him telling stories, chatting in bank lines, knowing everyone's name. I remembered the winter morning my mother ran into the house hysterical after finding a stranger sleeping in the backseat of our car. My father went out, chatted amicably with the man, and gave him a lift into town.

In short, it seems, my father taught me things good parents, in his day, never taught their kids. Always talk to strangers. Don't be careful. Go fast, take risks, have fun. Be creative. Surprise people. And never, ever worry about what they think of you. Whether or not my father intended his actions as examples, they turned out to be valuable lessons, and I'm grateful for them.

I suppose I should be angry at my father for never letting me get to know him. (He died in 1982, when I was twenty-two.) But I'm not. My father encouraged in me all the qualities that define me, the things about myself that I value and am proud of (and a few I'm not so proud of). He gave me my adventurousness and my independent streak, my optimism, my eccentricities, my creativity. Yes, I wish we'd been closer. I wish we'd felt comfortable talking to each other. I wish he'd been the kind of father who tells his children he loves them every day, or even the kind who tells them once a decade. But then I'd be wishing that my father had been a different person. And that's the last thing in the world I'd wish for.

AMY ALCOTT

■

Member, World Golf and LPGA Halls of Fame;
winner of five major championships and thirty-two
titles overall.

MY DAD WAS A MAN WHO NEVER let me know about restraints or obstacles. Thanks to him, I always thought that everything was possible. His name was Dr. Eugene Yale Alcott.

I grew up in Santa Monica in the sixties. I was a tomboy, and I was kidded a lot. The boys liked me well enough, and I could run as fast as most of them, but the girls didn't understand my gift. So I was a bit of a loner, and golf became my friend, my trusted companion. Day after day, I'd come home from school to chip and putt in our front yard.

My parents gave me my first cut-off golf club when I was eight. I'd seen a CBS Golf Classic, and I was fascinated. I asked my dad for a club and a ball and, to my surprise, he went to the closet and took out a set of clubs. He'd bought them for my mom when they got married, but neither of them played. My dad was a former handball champion; my mother, Lea, played very good tennis.

If I wanted to play golf, though, that was fine with him. My father was a striver, and on his own he'd graduated from Columbia University and then put himself through dental school. He brought our family to Santa Monica from Kansas City in 1956. He started a practice here and bought a home with a tennis court and swimming pool so that he could give us the California dream.

He had thought I'd choose tennis, but golf captivated me. He wanted to create an environment for athletics at our house, so when I outgrew pushing golf balls into sprinkler heads in our yard, and he realized that I was hooked on golf, he began construction of the "Alcott Golf and Country Club" right in our front yard, which I eagerly helped him design. We sank soup cans into the ground, and while he read the Sunday paper, I putted ball after ball. At night he held a flashlight for me, and I'd continue to putt until it was time for bed. Eventually, we went to a hardware store and got a real hole-cutting tool for the putting green. I can still remember him reading the directions. Next, he made me a bunker. We'd get bags of sand so that I could hit bunker shots onto the front yard. I broke a few windows, and he finally asked me if I could practice with plastic balls. When I told him I wouldn't, he installed a tall, huge net across our entire front yard, which made the neighbors shake their heads, I'm sure.

Most professional golfers grow up playing in country clubs. Thanks to my father's guidance and support, I was never envious of that, so every time I got invited to play at a country club, it was an exciting occasion. He knew that I had talent, and he began to enter me into all-boy tournaments. I remember he signed me up for a tournament at Fox Hills Golf Course, by the Los Angeles airport. I resisted because there were no girls playing. He encouraged me by telling me to just go out there with my pull cart and play eighteen holes and do the best that I could do. He told me to have a good time, and I was surprised to find I did.

He didn't want me to know about sexism, and perhaps he personally didn't even consider it an issue. He wanted me to play well and to win when I could. His greatest lesson was teaching me to follow my dreams, to honor every opportunity and not set any limits.

My parents divorced when I was in my early teens, and he became estranged from our family. He had a gambling problem, and we endured a lot of difficulties. I escaped into my golf. I lost contact with my father for many years, and during that time I compiled a successful junior record. I joined the LPGA Tour in 1975.

My dad eventually lost everything, but still he would show up at some of my tournaments. He was able to watch me win the U.S. Open in 1980, though he died six months later. I'll never forget seeing him in the gallery several times on the final day of the tournament, and how I felt that day as I walked up the 18th fairway and saw him under a tree, in sweltering 114-degree heat. At that moment, on that walk up to the 18th hole, I remember thinking, "He's the guy who built my sand trap and put up the net." As I was being driven to the press tent after the victory, we passed my dad, and I asked the driver to stop. I said, "He's my father, and he's going to ride with me."

We had breakfast together after that, for the first time in a very long time. Nothing seemed to have changed, even his old habit of putting a pat of butter and salt on his oatmeal. He had given me so much love and encouragement. As far as I am concerned, no one deserved more credit for my U.S. Open win than my father.

KRIS KRISTOFFERSON

■

Award-winning singer, songwriter, and actor whose songs include "Me and Bobby McGee" *and* "Help Me Make It Through the Night." *Recent inductee into the Country Music Hall of Fame.*

IN THE SUMMER OF 1958, I was deep in the catacombs in Rome, a little shabby after hitchhiking around Europe for a few months after graduating from college and before entering Oxford University, when I noticed a woman staring at me curiously. "Excuse me," she said. "Are you by any chance related to Henry Kristofferson?"

"He's my father," I said, amazed.

"I knew it!" she said. "You look so much like him!"

I thought of that some four decades later when my business manager (who's been with me nearly that long) said of the newest of my eight children, "He's got that Kristofferson look." So do my brother and sister, and so do their children. And so when I wish, as I often do, that my father were still alive for his grandchildren to enjoy, I realize that he's very much with us.

There's a picture of him with his brother and sister as children on the wall of the hallway in our home, along with the pictures of my children, as alike and as individually unique as snowflakes. And there is a picture of me as a toddler with him at the breakfast table, his arm around me while eating, uncannily like the way I have held my children.

He was born on August 16, 1906, the son of Swedish parents. His father was an officer in the Swedish army before emigrating to the United States and settling in Rainier, Washington, where he worked as a lumberjack. My mother told me that most of the population there was Irish, and that my father and his brothers got into fights at school over the "Little Lord Fauntleroy" Swedish clothing they wore (lace collars and such). Maybe that's how he got to be so good at boxing. (He was good at baseball, too.)

He realized his dream of becoming an aviator in the Army Air Corps Reserve and was on active duty when he and my mother were married in 1933. For some time afterward, he was a truck driver for an oil company, and then he became a pilot for Pan American Airways, flying to Central and South America out of Brownsville, Texas, where I was born in 1936. We lived for a while in Guatemala, in Florida, and New York, always returning to our home in Brownsville. His job kept him away from home a lot. He and his friend George Kraigher established several airfields in Africa that were used by the military during World War II.

When the United States entered the war, he was given sort of a battlefield commission, as either a major or a lieutenant colonel, and he received the Distinguished Flying Cross for being the first to fly over the Himalayas at night (without instruments), taking supplies to General Claire Chennault's Flying Tigers.

One of my happiest memories as a child is of climbing all over him with my sister, Karen, in a car that brought him from the airport during one of his few visits home during the war. (Nine months later my brother, Kraig, was born.)

After the war he was home for good, although his job as a pilot for Pan American kept him away a lot. In 1947, we moved to California, and during my adolescent years he had the uncomfortable responsibility of talking to me ("Wait 'til your father gets home!") after my mother gave him a report of my bad behavior during his absence. Despite this negative beginning to his times at home, we had a good relationship. He helped me with boxing (he was something on the speed bag), and I really respected him. He was the hardest worker I ever saw, clearing brush for my grandmother, doing yard work. I remember thinking I would never work that hard, even if I could. These days, my brother Kraig and I both enjoy the therapy of clearing out our land and hours on the tractor-mower.

He gave me some good words at some important times. He told me to "toughen up" once when I was feeling sorry for myself. "You'll feel better about yourself." He was right.

Although I'd seen news stories about my father's achievements—my mother showed me clippings full of praise and respect that included his promotion to major general in the air force after his service in the Korean War (he was in charge of the

Tokyo Airlift that flew the wounded to hospitals in Japan)—I
didn't know how special he really was until I met people who
had worked with him. When I was sixteen, I took a summer job
he got me in the Pan American mailroom at the San Francisco
airport. People at every job level made a point of telling me what
a good man my old man was. A year later I was on my way to
Wake Island to spend my summer working as a laborer for
Hawaiian Dredging (another job he got me), and every member
of the Pan Am crew told me how wonderful my father was.

Years after they both died, I read a letter from my dad to my
mom telling her how proud he was at my graduation from college and how different kinds of people kept coming up and
telling him what a wonderful son he had.

He died in his sleep on New Year's Day 1971, from a heart
condition that today would likely be correctable by an operation
similar to the triple bypass I had a few years ago. I was across
the country in Bearsville, near Woodstock, New York, with my
band, standing alone, outside in the dark in the snow, working
some song I was writing, when Bobby Neuwirth brought me the
news. I remember talking to my mother on the phone, and a
plane ride to California, but very little after that. I think I had
walking pneumonia at the time and was hospitalized shortly after rejoining my band for a tour that lasted—with brief inter-
ruptions to make some films—for several years without a break,
which kept me from dealing with the loss. It was several years
before I cried for the father I loved so deeply.

My father was a sharp, intelligent, capable man, with a

smile as warm as sunshine and a heart big enough to take on anything. I never saw a problem he couldn't handle, whether it was pulling my rain-soaked car out of the mud where I'd run it off the road and got stuck on Christmas night—he did it all in total silence—or taking over the management of the world's then-largest private airline, ARAMCO, in Saudi Arabia. And there were hidden acts of kindness. As a teenager, after I'd gotten into trouble with another kid over some stolen hubcaps, we were forbidden by the police to hang out together. My friend wrote me a letter years later saying that whenever my dad was in San Francisco, he had always gone from Pan Am over to United, where my old friend was working, to see if he was okay. Every trip. He did that for years, until they moved to Saudi Arabia.

He was an old-school good guy, behaving responsibly, an honest and loving husband and father, a highly respected citizen/soldier.

One of the last times I saw him, we were having a beer at the airport. I was just beginning to make a name for myself, working the clubs. He told me he didn't understand what I do—singing my songs for a living—but he could appreciate that I had to do it because no one could have told him not to fly.

I think of him more than ever these days. Like I said in the song "Don't Let the Bastards Get You Down," "I've just got to wonder what my daddy would have done if he'd seen the way they turned this dream around." I loved my father. And he loved me, and that's a wonderful gift to go off into the world with.

BETH KEPHART

■

Award-winning author of a memoir trilogy. Her first book, A Slant of Sun, *was a National Book Award finalist. Her fourth book,* Seeing Past Z, *was published in June 2004; her new book,* Ghosts in the Garden, *was recently released.*

THERE ARE PHOTOGRAPHS. MY FATHER, slim and auburn-haired, just sitting. My father (somewhat sheepish, almost proud) gone fishing. My father holding my only child's hand as they study some unknown miracle on the driveway. My father asleep in that house near the beach, after a morning of sun and counting dolphins. My father in photographs is good at doing little. But in life my father is something else again: He is good at doing much and seeking no one's praise for it.

We have the same body clock, my father and me. The same urge to rise in the hour before dawn, when the mind can hold a steady thought and nothing seems impossible. When I was a girl growing up, in the suburbs of Philadelphia, I would wake to the sound of my father's rising, wait for the smell of his toasted muffins and melted butter, listen for the snap of his briefcase (such a sound that was, such a pronouncement), then watch through the window as he drove away, his car's headlights singeing the darkness.

He wore good suits, well-ironed shirts, the ties my mother bought for him. He was the only one out on the streets at that hour, save perhaps for furry things. He didn't come back home until the world went dark again—the knot of his tie still up near his throat; the cuffs of his sleeves still buttoned, in place; his briefcase heavy with whatever he'd brought home to do that night, while we were sleeping. If our mother was always his best friend and advisor, we three kids knew little of the problems that our father encountered or solved, little of the play and pull of politics in his glassy office building. My father was an engineer who became a manager who eventually sat behind a desk on a corporation's upper floors. An oilman before he went into steel. An innovator of one sort or another. But what he did all day I don't think we kids ever really knew, for when he was home, he was our father, and he did not act like someone else.

Hey, Dad, how was work?
It was fine, Beth. How was school?
I still don't get the math. It's hard.
Bring your book, and we will do it.

I don't remember my father boasting. I don't remember any talk of sacrifice. I do remember that as I got older, I'd join him in the dark—come downstairs to the breakfast table, where it was just the two of us. Sometimes he would go over the tricks of algebra, trusting me to hold the rules of variables in my head. Sometimes he would ask me about my friends. Always he would proclaim that he made the best English muffins in the east, the only arrogance (he liked them charred, he liked the smoke above the toaster black) that he allowed himself. And then he would pack his briefcase and say good-bye and burn his headlights into the dissipating dark, leaving me awake to the dawn, my own thoughts in my head.

I was the middle child, and the first daughter. I was the one who would never lose my father's habit of rising early, in the dark. I am the age now that he was then, when we shared the breakfast table, and what I think about now, when I think about my dad, is how hard he surely worked and how little he'd speak of it. It was just muffins and butter, in that hour before dawn. It was just father and daughter, and the day, anticipated.

BEAU BRIDGES

■

Multiple Emmy and Golden Globe Award–winning
actor; member of the Bridges acting dynasty; father
and humanitarian.

"RESPECT," THAT'S THE WORD THAT resonates with me
when I think of my dad, which is often. I heard that
word a lot from him when I was growing up. I believe Lloyd
Bridges felt that respect for yourself, your fellow human beings,
and the planet that we live on should be our priorities. His own
life seemed an attempt to realize this ideal, and as much as it is
humanly possible, I think he achieved it.

"Faith" was also a major quality of my father's, and I'm
mostly talking about faith in his family. Here's a memory from
the summer of my tenth year, and I still can't figure out if my
dad's faith in me on that day so many years ago was of the blind
variety or not, and if it was "blind faith," did he do the right
thing?

I had just reached double digits and was probably dealing

with all the concerns most boys have about themselves as they look forward to young manhood. I was consumed with baseball at the time, and on a beautiful, hot Saturday afternoon, I was playing third base for the Angels in our Little League championship game. My dad was the head coach. I was a decent fielder and could hit the ball fairly well, but our team had made it to the finals mainly on the broad shoulders of our starting pitcher, Dicky. Coming to the bottom of the final inning (we played seven in those days), our team was relaxed; Dicky was throwing a shutout and had cruised through the first six innings, striking out most of the opposing batters, and now all he had to do was fan out the last three guys and we were the champs. But the heat had taken its toll on my buddy Dick, and after whiffing the first two batters, he walked the next three to load the bases. I wasn't too concerned; we had a comfortable lead, up by six runs.

I looked toward center field where Woody nervously pounded his hand into his mitt. He was a great pitcher in his own right, and I was sure our coach (my dad) would wave Woody in to take over for Dicky to get that last out, and we would all go home the champs. But no, Dad was not looking in Woody's direction; he was looking in mine. I had pitched a little during the season as the third pitcher in our rotation, usually when Dicky or Woody had to miss a game for one reason or another, but this was the finals. And there was my dad calling Dick off the mound and handing me the ball to go in and get that final out. I couldn't believe it! Why not let Dick tough it out? I knew he was fading, but we had a six-run lead and all he needed was one more out. And what about Woody? He was a year younger than Dick and I, but a tough kid with nerves of steel, and I knew he was ready and capable of doing the job. But no, Dad was handing the ball to me, saying, "Just throw strikes, son," and I took the mound.

My catcher, Bruce, showed me the target, and I swear his mitt looked like it was a hundred miles away. My whole body was shaking as I faced my first batter. I looked at my dad, and he gave me the thumbs-up sign. Well, I walked that first guy on four straight pitches. Score: six to one. I breathed deeply (Dad had told me to do that whenever I was nervous), and I threw my first strike to the next kid in the box, but four balls followed, and he trotted to first. Score: six to two. Okay, so what? All I needed was one out and I had three chances; surely I could do this, but I walked the next batter. Score: six to three. I looked again toward center where Woody was furtively kicking the grass with his cleats. I had walked three guys; surely Dad would bring in Woody, who would get the final out, and my poor performance would be forgotten by my teammates as we hugged each other in congratulations. But no, the coach was just looking at me calmly with this easy smile on his face. So I walked the next four batters. Tie score: six to six. How could my dad do this to me, to our team? I begged him with my eyes to take me out, but that easy smile said, "No." So I did my best with the kid who eagerly opposed me at the plate. I took him to a full count, then walked him, too. The final run scored; we had lost seven to six. I had walked seven straight batters.

I was devastated that day, humiliated, and I was angry at my father. I couldn't talk to him about it for days, maybe weeks . . . months. Later in my life, after I had children of my own and our relationship had mellowed (he had become my best friend as well as my father), I loved to tease and taunt him about his coaching decision. "How could you have done this to your son? The damage you did to me on that day was irreparable. . . ." and so on. He never took the bait. His reply was always a simple chuckle, followed by that big, easy smile of his.

Blind faith? Maybe so. Unconditional love from a parent to a child? Definitely. I still can't quite figure it out. But I'll tell you this, if I were Dicky or Woody or any of the other guys on our team, I would have been pissed.

Maybe it had something to do with respect. You know, his wanting me to know how much he respected me as his son, or maybe it was his attempt to drum up in me some measure of respect for myself. Whatever it was, I don't think it had anything to do with winning or losing. It was just a moment between a father and his son . . . that will last a lifetime.

TAMARA TUNIE

■

Recurring roles on both Law and Order: SVU, *on* NBC, *and the daytime drama* As the World Turns, *on CBS. During the first season of* 24, *Tunie commuted from New York to Los Angeles weekly to work on all three shows. Other credits include* Sex and the City *and* NYPD Blue *and films such as* The Devil's Advocate, The Caveman's Valentine, *and* Snake Eyes. *Tunie starred in the Broadway revival of* Oh Kay! *and in the first African American production of* Cat on a Hot Tin Roof, *among other theater work.*

I GREW UP IN A FUNERAL HOME. My dad, James Waddy Tunie, Sr., had essentially two full-time jobs for as long as I can remember. He was a skycap for many years with TWA. He is also a licensed mortician, and when I was about three years old, we moved to Homestead, Pennsylvania, and he established his own business there. We lived above the funeral home in a big house like in *Six Feet Under*. It's very similar: lots of woodwork, three stories, with the morgue in the basement. When I first saw the show, I said, "Oh, wait—that's our house."

I had a brother and three sisters, and there were people and kids coming and going all the time. Whenever there was a viewing or a funeral, we would have to be very quiet upstairs, no rough-housing or teasing each other. But it's what I knew from birth, so it was normal for us.

My dad helped put all five of us through college. We just celebrated his seventy-seventh birthday, and he still has the funeral home. My mom always said that he is the best funeral director she knows. (She is also a licensed mortician, and they continue to work together, even though they divorced after all the kids were grown.) He's a great reconstructive artist: Sometimes people die tragically or horribly, and he has to do some reparation before he can lay the body out. And he's good with the bereaved. He's very dignified but at the same time very accessible to and caring with the grieving families.

When I was young, there was a family with whom we were good friends. The mother's sister's house caught fire, and two of the children were killed. They called my father to do a double funeral; you can imagine how emotional that was. I'm getting choked up just thinking about it. We knew these kids because when they came over to play with their cousins, we all played together, so it was almost like losing family for us. I remember the parents coming to the funeral home, and the mom, who was distraught, naturally, really falling apart. My dad stepped in and consoled her, but he wasn't intrusive in their grief. While conducting business, he could still be so comforting.

My dad was also very funny—not in those situations, of

course—I used to love when his friends would stop by, and they'd have coffee at the kitchen table, and I would just sit down and listen to them exchange stories and laugh. He isn't a joke teller; his humor is off-the-cuff and based on the situation. One time, my older sister, Linda, and my younger sister, Stacy, and I were having a race in the house. Stacy was always kind of a chubby kid, and when she reached puberty, everything shifted to all the right places, so at thirteen she became relatively well endowed. My dad loves to go to the racetrack; he likes the horses and the dogs. So he was doing a kind of running commentary on our race, and Stacy moved ahead of us, and out of nowhere he said, "Yes, and Tilly Tits has taken the lead." Of course, Stacy was horrified, but the rest of us just fell apart. "Dad!"

My dad's mother is Native American; in fact, we have Native American on both sides. He couldn't dance to save his life, and any time some music played, he would launch into a sort of powwow, Indian-stomp dance that we always found funny. I mean, we grew up with the sounds of Motown and the great bands of seventies soul and funk! I call us the epitome of an American family because our ancestors are from Africa, Europe, and this native land; we really are the mixed bag of Americanism. We have all of that in our heritage, and it expresses itself in different ways at different points in our lives. Of course, when it comes to the census, we're black. As far as stereotypes go, though, let's just say my father has *no* rhythm.

He had a bit of a belly, and when I was little, that was my favorite place to take a nap. I would crawl up on his stomach and suck my thumb and go to sleep. But we didn't see a lot of him when he was doing the 3 to 11 p.m. shift at TWA. We only saw him on his days off, and sometimes those would be filled with funerals. He would get extremely busy during the holidays, from Thanksgiving to the new year. So his time with us was limited, to say the least, but it was always quality time.

For years, we had a special routine if I was awake when he came home from the airport. As he was coming up the steps to the second floor—we had a beautiful staircase like in *Six Feet Under*—he would say, "Who loves you?" and I would answer, "You do." He would say, "How much?" and I would say, "A bushel and a peck and a hug around the neck." And then I'd throw myself into his arms and give him a big hug around the neck.

JOSH KORNBLUTH

Berkeley-based monologuist (Red Diaper Baby, Ben Franklin: Unplugged, Love & Taxes) *and filmmaker* (Haiku Tunnel).

I N RETROSPECT, IT WAS THE LAST summer of my childhood. By the fall, I would be living away from home for the first time—out of New York City at last, and beginning college in far-off New Jersey. And not long after that, my father would suffer the debilitating stroke that made his few remaining years a time of shadows and averted glances.

But on this long, hot weekend in the mid-seventies, my father, Paul Kornbluth, and I were together—healthy, exuberant, and in pursuit of one of our mutual passions: folk music. I didn't know which prospect excited me more: the opportunity to see legendary folksingers like Dave Van Ronk at the Philadelphia Folk Festival, or the fact that we'd be staying at the Holiday Inn. Oh, how I loved Vibrato-Beds in those days! Maybe it had something to do with me still being a virgin at the time, but the idea that you had merely to drop in a quarter and your bed would start vibrating filled me with something like euphoria.

We arrived at our hotel in suburban Philadelphia early on Saturday morning. (The festival's name was somewhat misleading, as the event actually took place several miles outside the city.) My father—an avid swimmer back in his college days—was thrilled to find that we had scored a poolside suite. As I deposited a quarter and settled in for a few minutes of relaxing bed-vibration, Dad threw on some trunks and headed out to the pool.

Seconds later, the whole area resounded with the depth-charge sound of my father doing a cannonball into the water. He was a very large man, and he made a very big splash. Some moments after that, his voice boomed out, commanding me to join him.

With some reluctance, I rolled out of my comforting, womblike Vibrato-World, changed into trunks, and made my way out to the pool. My dad had recently paid for me to take some private swimming lessons, and (as was his wont) he had assumed that I was now a Mark Spitz–level swimmer. This was part of a pattern: In my father's eyes, I was dynamic, fearless, a winner—kind of a Jewish James Bond. In truth, I was a nerd and a wimp—fearful of the physical world to the point of paranoia.

As Dad merrily did laps on his back—his enormous splashes causing those at poolside to slide their tanning chairs a few feet farther away—I gingerly began descending an aluminum ladder into the heavily chlorinated water. I could do this: My swimming had progressed to the point where I could manage to back-float from one side of a pool to the other. I would do a lap, then—having satisfied my father that I was indeed now like a fish of the sea—would retreat back to the Vibrato-Comfort of our suite.

But my dad had other ideas: "No, no, my son—you must dive in!"

A Kornbluth man, you see, did not make a wishy-washy entrance. A Kornbluth man leapt into the fray. And I was a Kornbluth man.

I allowed myself a small, private sigh and stepped off the ladder and back onto the side of the pool. There was nothing to be done about it: Dad wanted me to dive, so I had to dive. I made my way around the edge of the pool and climbed the few steps up onto the diving board. I walked out to the edge.

Dad was treading water at the other end of the pool, watching me with his usual loving expectancy. His booming shouts had by now drawn a crowd. After all, such a hullabaloo must indicate the appearance of some Olympian! Perhaps this chubby young man (me) was the next championship diver who would bring back gold for America.

But the truth was, I had never dived before. Not ever. I had tried once, years earlier, at summer camp. I had stood at the edge of the diving board at that camp pool—staring, staring down into the watery depths—and had been unable to convince myself that once I'd plunged down forcefully into the water, I'd ever come back up. It just didn't make sense. All I could envision was that my blobby body would sink down to the bottom and then stay there, forever—something for future campers to visit and, eyes wide with wonder, examine before resurfacing. The counselor yelled at me; other kids jeered; but I could not jump. Eventually I had gotten down on my hands and knees and somehow lowered myself slowly into the water below the diving board.

Now, though, the stakes were higher. Now, with my father waiting for me—*expecting* me—to execute a swift and confident dive into the Holiday Inn pool, it seemed that my manhood was on the line.

I stared down into the water. It looked deep. It looked watery. It looked unsupportive.

"Come on, Joshy!" Dad yelled. He was in a fine mood, and seemed to assume that—with an audience watching—I was pausing only to milk this moment for its inherent dramatic value. "Jump, my son!"

I considered my immediate future. It clearly was within my power to dive into the water. All I had to do was lean forward—release myself—allow gravity to take me down, down, down.

But would there be an up? Intellectually, I knew there probably would, but that wasn't helping me to send the "dive" command to my recalcitrant body.

The crowd around the pool was joining in the merriment. "Jump! Jump! Jump!" they began chanting, along with my dad.

The sun was baking my pale, city-boy's shoulders. It would be so much cooler down there in the water. And my dad wouldn't be staring at me anymore down there in the water. And I would have proved myself to him, and to the Holiday Inn community.

I remember when Dad's expression changed—when he seemed to realize that I was not playing, not goofing around. That I was truly terrified. And at that moment, as I gazed out helplessly at him from my perch, I saw something in his eyes that I had never seen before: the recognition that I was not the smashing, self-assured success he had always assumed I was. That his dream—the dream that had kept him afloat through many terrible, self-recriminating years after my parents' divorce—the dream that his son would stride the world unafraid, conquering all that lay before him—that dream was gone.

Eventually, I simply turned and walked off the diving board, then back into our suite. Dad joined me a few minutes later. We sat there in the darkness—him on a chair, me lying facedown on the bed.

I was out of quarters.

BILLIE JEAN KING

For five years ranked #1 women's tennis player in the world; winner of six Wimbledon championships and four U.S. Open titles; defeated Bobby Riggs in the September 20, 1973, televised Battle of the Sexes. First woman athlete to win more than $100,000; Sports Illustrated's first female Sportsperson of the Year (1972). Selected by LIFE magazine as one of the "100 most important Americans of the 20th century."

BILL MOFFITT WAS A JOCK, an all-around athlete. His first love was basketball, and he was very good in track-and-field. He also loved baseball; for a while he was a scout for the Milwaukee Brewers. Before I was born, my dad was in the navy's training facility in Norfolk, Virginia. He was a physical trainer for the guys going over to Europe during World War II. My mom said, "I'm going to name my baby after him, just in case something happens." Otherwise, I would have been called Michelle Louise or something like that.

We didn't see each other for the first two years of my life.

When he finally came home and walked in the door, I wasn't shy. I didn't cling to my mother. I said, "Daddy, Daddy" and rushed to him with my arms outstretched. Our strong bonding had begun.

He became a police officer, but he didn't like it because he didn't have the heart to give out tickets. Then he became a firefighter, work he absolutely loved. He drove the fire engine that got the water to the fire; that was his job. He kept it so clean you could eat off it. And firefighters always commented on his good eye. They would tell me about the time he drove down an alley with one inch on each side of the truck. The guys were sweating it out, but he just drove right through. He knew he'd get there faster, and that was important. He worked out down at the firehouse, and they would laugh at him because most of the guys didn't work out then. It was twenty-four hours on and twenty-four hours off, so he was home every other night, and when he was home, he always spent his time with us.

My mother says that my brother, Randy, who is nearly five years younger, and I were *always* moving—first in the womb, then as soon as we got out. We were both crazed for anything to do with a ball. I wanted to play all the time, and my dad was very patient with me. He'd play catch with me forever, from the time I was very young. I can't remember a time when we didn't play, and he was an excellent teacher. My dad understood fitness and wanted us to get that lesson as kids; he understood that keeping active is essential. And I'll never forget his standing up for me when I wanted to play out in the streets with the boys, and they wouldn't let me because I was a girl. He told them to give me a chance, that I'd hold my own, and I did.

In fifth grade, my friend Susan Williams invited me to play tennis, and I asked her, "What's tennis?" My parents didn't play, and I didn't know anything about it. She took me to her country club—I'd never been to such a place—and I got on the court and tried to hit balls with her. Then when I was ten or eleven, I had my first free group tennis lesson in a park, and I loved it. I made up my mind then that I wanted to be the best in the world.

I started playing tournaments, and my parents would always ask how it went. I was a perfectionist, very self-critical, especially when I didn't win. My dad would ask, "Did you try your best?" and I would answer, "Well, of course." And then he'd say, "That's good enough," and I'd say, "No, it's not. I lost." And he'd repeat, "It's *good enough*."

When I was about twelve years old, I was ranked #2 in my division in Long Beach. Well, I wanted to be #1 in the world. He explained, "You're kind of a big fish here, but you realize that when you start to go to these sectional tournaments, you'll be meeting kids from all over Southern California, and you'll see how the competition gets better. Then you have to think about state and then national competition; if you talk about the world, that's even bigger. So you are talking about a lot of heartache and how tough it can be." He was so great, the way he tried to give me the big picture. Most kids have a dream for a week or two and then move on. I explained to him that this was what I wanted to do with my life. But the talk helped. He made me understand that if I really wanted this, it would be rough, though that didn't deter me at all. It got me more excited.

I also remember once, when I acted like a bad sport, he took me out to the garage with my racket, picked up a power saw, and told me he was going to cut it in half. He wasn't a great sport himself, so I thought that was amusing. My dad had a very competitive nature when he played sports. I saw him in a night-league basketball game with the fire department when he was forty-two years old. He was just crazed, so intense—a maniac, really. John McEnroe had nothing on him, believe me.

Today, too many tennis parents, and other parents, push their kids too hard, torment their children, try to live through them. Not mine. My father gained a lot of dignity from my brother and me doing so well—Randy became a professional baseball player with the San Francisco Giants—but it was also difficult for my parents. My dad took a second job, and my mother started selling Tupperware and Avon so that we could live our dreams.

The tougher part for them was that they had to share us with the world when we were young. We weren't around that much. They didn't like to travel, and during all my years on the pro tour, they never went to the U.S. Open. I had to beg to get them to Wimbledon once, in 1968. They were there for my victory over Bobby Riggs. But most of the time, they watched me on TV. They're very proud of both of us, and sometimes they still shake their heads thinking that their daughter wanted to be #1 in tennis and their son wanted to be a major league baseball player, and it all happened.

When we were growing up, there was a lot of swing dancing in our house. My brother and I loved to watch our parents dance and applaud them. They are in their eighties now, living in Arizona, and they'll go dancing once or twice a week. I see them as often as possible, and sixty years later, I'm still cheering them on.

ROBERT MONDAVI

Napa Valley pioneer, founder of the Robert Mondavi Winery, and creator of COPIA, the American Center for Wine, Food & the Arts.

IN TERMS OF PHYSICAL STATURE, my father was not a big man. In fact, he was so short that he could barely see over the steering wheel of his car—and other drivers could barely see him. The joke in the Napa Valley was that if you saw a car rolling down the road without a driver, it must belong to Cesare Mondavi.

To me, though, Dad was a giant. My mother taught us to appreciate good food and good wine and the family warmth and togetherness that are nurtured best at the family table. Dad was a more remote and demanding figure, but he was a wonderful father to me, my brother, Peter, and our sisters, Mary and Helen. He taught us great lessons about life and the best values to have and protect.

My father and my mother, Rosa, came from hardworking

families. They grew up on the hillsides outside of Sassoferrato, a farming and mining town in central Italy, a few hours' drive south of Venice. Life was tough. Their families had been share-croppers for generations. They lived in primitive stone farm-houses, with no heat or electricity, and they had small plots of land on which they cultivated wheat and vegetables and raised rabbits and chickens. They were obliged to give about half of whatever they produced to the man who owned the land, who lived in a fancy manor house on the top of their hill.

In the early 1900s that part of Italy was in a terrible depres-sion, and my father and his older brother decided to try their luck in the iron ore mines of northern Minnesota. It was rough work, but the pay was better than in Italy, so my father went back, married Rosa, and brought her to Minnesota. When his brother was killed in a mining accident, Dad decided to find an-other line of work. He and Mom were running a boardinghouse for the Italians who had come to work in the mines, and then they added another business: a small Italian grocery and saloon. Both of them worked like slaves, and the winters were brutal. In the early 1920s Dad saw a brighter future for us, and he and Mom packed us up and moved the family west to Lodi, in Cali-fornia's fertile Central Valley. There, Dad launched himself into something new: the wholesale fruit and grape business.

As a kid I helped load the trucks and nail together the wooden boxes we used for shipping the grapes. I got paid by the hour, plus a small bonus for every box I nailed, and over the years I was able to put a good bit of money into the bank. And it's a damn good thing I did. One day Dad came to me with a grave expression on his face. The Depression, he explained, had hit the family hard. Very hard. He needed money desperately, and he had nowhere else to turn. So he asked me, "Bobby, can I borrow that money you've saved?" Dad was a very positive man, and he knew things would get better; we just had to continue to work hard and think smart. Besides, he had been through far worse back in Italy. He made me a promise: "Not only will I pay you back in full, Bobby, but I'll send you to any university you want to go to."

Well, Dad was able to steer us through those terrible Depression years, and he was true to his word. Of course I had to choose the most expensive school, Stanford. The cost was a burden; we were just getting back on our feet. But he had made me a promise, and by golly he was going to keep it.

On that beautiful campus in Palo Alto, I studied economics, accounting, business administration, marketing, sales, financial planning—and by junior year, I thought I knew a thing or two about how to sell, how to build a client base, negotiate deals, and build a business. In fact, I was pretty full of myself (and many people say I still am!), but Dad soon showed me how little I actually knew. One day he said, "Bobby, I'm going on a little business trip. Why don't you come along?" I said, "Sure," thinking maybe I'd at least see how business was done the old-fashioned Italian way.

We took the train to Chicago and then on up to Virginia, Minnesota, where Dad had started out in the mines and in the grocery business. We went east to New York, New Jersey, and Boston. And everywhere we went, Dad met up with old friends in the wine and food business. Many of them were Italian, but many were not. In each place, Dad and his friends played cards, they played bocce, they ate fabulous dinners, and they always had a wonderful time. I kept waiting for them to sit down and talk business, but you know what? They never did! Just before it was time for us to get on the train, one of his clients would say to my father, "Well, Cesare, my friend, last year we took so many loads of grapes and we did this much business." They'd discuss the quality of this year's grape crop and how this year's prices were shaping up. They'd air any problems they foresaw, and then they'd place their orders and quickly agree to a price. And that was it! That was the full extent of their business discussion and negotiations!

I was amazed—and perplexed. At Stanford I had studied all sorts of business models, but I had never seen anything like this. Play bocce, eat spaghetti, and drink wine? That to me was not doing business; it was having a good time! Something else struck me on that trip: My father never got angry or even argumentative. In fact, I saw that he hated confrontation. One day we sat down with a grape grower and it became clear that the man was trying to chisel my father. I was furious and ready to pound the table, determined to defend our interests and call the man out. But not Dad. He just stood up politely and walked away. If a man had no integrity, Dad wanted nothing to do with him. That was simply *not* the way he wanted to do business.

What slowly dawned on me was that for my father there was

no difference between business and friendship. He and his clients were partners in the deepest sense: If Dad prospered, he wanted his friends to prosper, too. They were in business together, through the good times and the rough times. Mother Nature always has a say in the fruit and grape business; one bad frost can ruin an entire crop—and wipe out a farmer for an entire year. When that happens, you want to know that your business partners are people who will stand by you and give you a helping hand. In my father's world, there were no long negotiations, no contracts, no lawyers. All deals were sealed with a handshake. He and his friends understood each other, they trusted each other, they were like family, and their word was their bond. Business trips were not about cutting deals; they were about renewing and strengthening friendships.

What I learned at Stanford, of course, had its place, too. But on that trip with my father, I learned much deeper truths. Business, I finally came to see, was not, first and foremost, about money and profit. It was about integrity and trust. It was about honesty and fairness. If you wanted to succeed, you first had to prove yourself to be a loyal friend. Above all, you had to be true to your word. What you need first in business is not a fancy logo or a catchy marketing slogan; you need the kind of reputation where the people you deal with will say, "Oh, so-and-so? His word is as good as gold." That was the essential truth on which I went on to build my own life in the wine business, and I learned it quietly and effectively from the best teacher I ever had, my dad.

WINSTON GROOM

■

Author of Forrest Gump *and numerous other books including* Conversations with the Enemy *(with Duncan Spencer), a finalist for the 1984 Pulitzer Prize for fiction; his most recent book is* 1942: The Year That Tried Men's Souls.

WE HAD BEEN MARRIED NEARLY ten years, but no baby. My friends' children were grown or growing up, and Anne-Clinton's friends were all beginning to hatch broods of little ones. She would drop hints from time to time, the most heartbreaking when she would see some toy or child's thing at a store and say, "Oh, wouldn't that be precious for our baby. . . ." I am aware of many faults and flaws in my character, but breaking hearts isn't one of them, and so I set out to give her her baby.

In due time, on a breathtaking autumn morning high in the mountains of North Carolina, she said to me, very quietly, "I think I'm pregnant." For me it was a moment of divine complexity. "That's wonderful! Wonderful!" I shouted, falling into her arms, but at the same time there was a strange mixed feeling I couldn't quite decipher: a child, another human in the family, and the cry rang out in my head like the disturbing fragment of some long-forgotten dream, "It will change your life forever!"

Thing was, I didn't want my life changed forever; the very notion of it is frightening. Having a child would not be like buying a dog. There would be diapers and babysitters and crying and health scares and . . . well, soccer. But at the same time I was, of course, gratified and elated and did my best to shove my craven selfishness back to where it came from.

In due time—nine months almost precisely—Carolina Montgomery Groom arrived in the world in a delivery room at a hospital near our home in Point Clear, Alabama. I was present at the delivery, a notion that would have horrified women of my mother's generation. It horrified me, too, for a while, but Anne-Clinton insisted. I'm glad she did, if for no other reason than to witness the glistening tears of joy in her eyes and sweet smile on her face when the nurse handed Carolina to her to hold for the first time. A dozen of our friends were in the waiting room outside, and I heard the cheer go up all the way down the hall as soon as somebody announced, "It's a girl!"

Secretly, I was happy it was a girl. Anne-Clinton (everybody calls her AC) is femininity personified, and I knew there would be a bonding between the two of them beyond the power of words. And besides, I was relieved that I wouldn't have to be playing touch football at age sixty-five or seventy with a big moose of a son. In any event, that's when it all started, like the chorus from *The Trojan Women*: "It will change your life forever!"

The years since have passed so quickly, life seems to have

become like one of those time-lapse pictures of a growing flower. I look back with an unutterable fondness on the mornings I would be working in my office, and Carolina would crawl in to sit on my lap—then her first steps, and then she was walking; her first words, whatever they were; and since then she never sits down and never shuts up, which is okay by me. I adore her. For her first birthday I bought her a big fancy rocking horse that apparently had been taken from an old carousel. It took two men to deliver it into the house, and when AC saw me standing proudly beside it, she burst out laughing. "Heavens," she said, "she'll be three years old before she can get up on that thing!"

Carolina Montgomery, who is named for her great-great-great-grandmother, began school, nursery school, when she was three, at the Hampton School in the little village of Cashiers, North Carolina. It was a red-letter day, watching her toddle off into the schoolhouse, lunch pail in hand, escorted by her teacher. The whole way in she was looking back nervously at her Papa, who was waving wistfully from the car. She was growing up. AC threw a big birthday party that year, with magicians and strolling minstrels and clowns and a pony for the kids to ride. Carolina was terrified of the pony, a fact that pleased me, because I had not particularly looked forward to a lifetime of horses, and everything that entails.

Naturally, I was wrong. The next year she began riding fearlessly on an Irish pony belonging to some friends, and now the discussion in the house often centers not on if but *when* she is going to get her first horse.

Until she was nearly six, Carolina could not swim, she just floundered around, a fact that alarmed me because we have a large swimming pool; but at the same time I secretly hoped this development might lead to an aversion to water, with all of water's attendant dangers. Fat chance. Once we dragged her into swimming lessons at the beginning of her sixth summer, she took to water like a duck and began winning swimming meets all over coastal Alabama. She's got a backstroke like a paddle wheel steamboat and a wall full of trophies to prove it.

There isn't anything she won't try or do. Soccer (of course), T-ball, tennis, gymnastics, violin and piano lessons—and, of course, the horses. There has been trauma, of course, and heartbreak, too. When it was decided that her tonsils had to come out, we all went to the hospital before dawn, and outside the operating room I encountered the anesthesiologist.

"I want you to be with her at all times," I said, recalling horror stories of doctors who would put a patient under and then go off down the hall to do something else. Seeing the fierce look on my face, he instantly agreed. When Carolina came out of the operating room, they put her in a private room, and when we went in, there was blood all over her mouth and chin, and she seemed to be gagging. I immediately hit the panic button and ran screaming down the hall for a nurse. When I got back, AC was sitting beside her, calmly wiping off the blood with Kleenex.

"Take it easy," she said, "kids have their tonsils out all the time."

That same year there was tragedy. Carolina was on her way

with AC to ballet lessons when AC inadvertently backed over and killed the little toy poodle we had. Carolina loved that dog— we all did—and was strapped in the backseat when it happened. She didn't know the dog was dead then, only that something bad had happened. Everybody was terribly upset. I said I would drive her to the ballet class because AC wasn't in any shape to do so, and Carolina didn't need to be there just then. I think I will never forget her feeble words as we left the driveway, they were so full of hurt, fear, and pathos: "Papa, why is Mommy crying?"

What happens next I don't know, and won't until it happens. Every day there is some new phrase that startles you, some fresh understanding you never expect. "Papa," she asked one day, "when I get to heaven, will I be with Gobbie?" which was the name of the little dog that was killed.

"Why, sure, honey," I told her. "She'll be there."

"But what if I can't find her?" she said.

So now it's first grade, and then there'll be second and third and so on and then the boys. Looking forward, I could kick my-self over the stupid and mean-spirited thoughts I had when she was afraid of horses. If the horses can keep her from the boys—if only for a few more years—life will be conspicuously less trying.

As I write this, I see the car pulling into the drive. Carolina has been to some lesson or other. Soon I'll hear the joy of run-ning feet, and she'll appear at my office door, as if by magic— and believe me, it is magic: "Papa, can we play checkers?"

Yeah, my life has changed forever! Yeah!

ANN CURRY

Co-anchor, news reporter, the Today *show.*

M Y FATHER'S NAME IS Robert Paul Curry, and he was a chief petty officer in the navy. The navy was his ticket to a life outside of working at the steel mill in Pueblo, Colorado, the only job available for a kid like him, a poor boy raised by a single mother. The war broke out; he was excited about doing something for his country; he joined the military. Later, he would have to go off on these three-month, six-month, tours of duty, and because he has always been such a huge force in my life, I remember how I missed him.

And I can remember opening the screen door and seeing a flash of light and then seeing the LONNNNGGGG legs of my six-foot-three father, and his dress whites, and making the turn and seeing his face. And that burst of joy—that incredible feeling when every nerve is tingling, every happy and joyful emotion exploding—and running into his arms, and that is my first memory.

The story of how my parents married has given me a great legacy of love and courage. At the end of World War II, my father was sent to Japan to be part of the occupation force. My mother was a poor rice farmer's daughter. She had traveled into the city to help her family survive, because they hadn't had any seed to grow rice during the war years, and there was great hunger in her family. Her cousin got her a job punching tickets on a streetcar. One day this very tall, green-eyed man got on the streetcar, and he wouldn't get off; he kept riding and riding, and so she took notice of him. She was four foot eleven in a kimono—as Japanese as one can imagine in terms of how she thought and how she looked, and on top of that, she was from rural Japan, as old-country as one could get. Eventually, when he asked to take her to go eat noodles, she figured out that he was riding the streetcar because he had taken a fancy to her. She finally agreed to go with a girlfriend to meet him.

They were both eighteen years old, kids. He had just joined the military; she had just left the farm. They fell in love and he asked her to marry him, and she said yes. But the military told him if he married her, his eyes would start to slant and he would turn into a "bamboo American." They were trying to protect him from a rash decision, they thought, at a very young age. So rather than let him marry, the military immediately sent him to Morocco. He had a couple of days, and he went to her and told her what had happened. She described being at the train station and him telling her, "I'm coming back," and her saying, "You

2

guys never come back; I'm never going to see you again." And then watching the train go and walking into the train station and sitting down on the bench and sobbing and sobbing, knowing that she had said good-bye to her one true love, forever.

They didn't see each other for two years. He wrote and sent money to her family, still struggling in Japan. But he had met somebody on a ship in Morocco who was going to Washington, D.C., and he asked him to hand-carry some transfer-request papers to Washington, and eventually Daddy got his papers to go back to Japan. He went to her mother's house, and her mother answered the door and called my mother from the other room. And there was this big, tearful reunion, but then he realized as he was holding her that she was so incredibly small—skeletal. She told him that she had been diagnosed with a terminal case of tuberculosis.

The military wasn't letting men marry women who had tuberculosis, so her sister took the X-ray; they got her sister's documents, and they got married; and then my mother had surgery through a joint operation with the American and Japanese doctors. They took out ninety percent of one of her lungs, and she survived. My father nursed her back to health for months. And her mother, who was against the marriage, finally told her, "You will never find a man who will love you this much—change your bedpans and wash you clean every day while you're sick—I bless your marriage." They were married until the day my mother died, nearly fifty years, and I'm the oldest of their five kids.

My father is the biggest influence of my life, primarily because his message to me was so positive from day one. He told me, "Ann, you're the best of both worlds. You never have to choose, you never have to feel ashamed of your ancestors. That your mother and I saw through our prejudices to fall in love and despite all odds stay together—you should be proud of that." And he would say to me regularly when I was growing up, "So, Ann, when are you going to run for president?" He was saying that there is nothing you cannot achieve.

He would argue with me about the events of that day. We would get into these huge, emotional discussions about the world and what was happening in it. That made me think outside my small town in Ashland, Oregon, and my small family. It is the reason I am a journalist today, because he planted the seeds of a huge interest in the world and our part in it. I received a letter just last week that said, "Ann, when are you going to run for president?" He is still letting me know there is no end; there is no stopping.

When I was younger, he said something quintessential in terms of my sense of what's right and what's wrong: "Whatever you do in life, remember to do something that's in service to others. It could be your job; it could be as a human being, a neighbor, a friend, a wife, a mother. Do something of service to others because then, at the end of your days, you'll know that it mattered that you were born." What a gift to give your children, the opportunity to look outside themselves—to realize from a young age that it's not about whether their jeans are right or whether they are popular, and to learn that early enough so that they can make a choice.

I have a kind of worship for my father because I am so grateful. Given how hard life was, the fact that he never had a father, that he rose despite that and through poverty to fall in love and deal with racism, to raise five children on a meager military salary, to contend with the fact that we didn't have that much, and with the fact that we were the only multiracial people we knew—with all that, he helped us prepare for the future and gave us hope that our future was not limited. Moreover, he taught us that it's not about money or fame; it's about having a life of significance. How could I not worship this man?

And he created the life of significance that he taught us to have. He had joined the military because he wanted to do something for his country, but his real dream was to be a teacher. He taught junior high school kids—the most difficult age, I think, to teach; he taught physical education and health, and he became a coach. He thought then and he still thinks that you teach by example—to be an honorable person, to be someone whom others may want to emulate. That's how he taught me, and that's how he taught his students. He still has people come up to him and say, "Mr. Curry, do you remember me? I was in your seventh-grade class, and this is what you said to me, and I'll never forget it."

I married at the age of thirty-three—relatively late, I guess, but I had a high standard to measure against. I didn't want to waste my time with someone who didn't have that kind of goodness in them. My husband, Brian, and my dad are the kind of people who, if they see someone drowning, will run to save that person, even if it's someone they don't know. Martin Luther King struck a chord with all of us for many reasons, but one of the things he said that resonated with me was about being judged by the content of our character. If you measured my dad or my husband by the content of their character, you would be stunned.

My father influences my mothering dramatically because he taught me every chance he could about what really matters in life. When I talk to my children when they're faced with a difficulty, I think about what my father would say. It's not just "Oh, feel better"; it's "How do you really feel about this? And do you understand there are people whose suffering is far greater?" The idea is to teach them not just about being grateful but also about empathizing with others who have more to worry about. About the idea of service, and of trying to understand. My daughter's eleven now, and my son is nine, and we are having passionate debates just as I did with my father. In so many ways, he is present in my home.

And when they go see my dad, it's like a homecoming every time, because they hear from him exactly what they hear from me. What matters in the end is what kind of person you were. Did you do your best, did you love enough, were you presented with a chance to do good, did you take it? That's ultimately the life I strive for, and it's all because of my father.

OSCAR MAXIMILLIAN TUCCI

Pursues both philanthropic and creative ventures; has donated time and money to organizations from the Montefiore Children's Hospital in the Bronx to the American Ballet Theatre, and supports many private charities. He was a fashion and lifestyle expert on Tyra Banks's UPN reality show America's Next Top Model *and featured on the WE (Women's Entertainment) channel's* Young, Sexy, Royal *(January '05). With his sister, Nicoletta, he is working to open a restaurant called Oscar's Delmonico Cafe.*

I'M NAMED FOR BOTH MY grandfathers and my father, Mario Carlo Tucci. My full name is Oscar Maximillian Mario Carlo Julius Tucci. My grandfather Oscar came here from Florence, Italy, in the early twenties and took over Delmonico's. The restaurant, which is at Beaver and South William in Manhattan's Wall Street area, originated in 1827, but my grandfather made it into a place where celebrities would come, and diplomats, and princes and kings—the whole high-society world. As time went on, it grew to serve eight hundred lunches a day. The building was enormous, roughly seventy thousand square feet with three or four floors of dining and, upstairs, private clubs like the Bulls Club and the Bears Club—a fun gathering place for businessmen. At night, it drew a more glamorous crowd.

My father took it over after my grandfather passed away, and he kept the legend going. It was the perfect business for him because he loved entertaining people. He always wanted new people to come in, new faces—to keep it a beautiful, social place where everyone was welcome. It was geared toward society and wealthier people, and obviously the menu prices reflected that, but if someone was down and came to the restaurant stairs, my father would take them in and set a table up for them.

He wore blazers and ascots, and his shoes were always perfectly polished. He taught me that you can always tell a man by his shoes and cars. If you have time to clean your shoes and your cars, you are living life right. If your shoes and cars are dirty, you have too many things going on, and you need to focus more on yourself and your home. Though he dressed like an English gentleman, he was Italian, so, of course, he cooked a lot. He was an amazing chef. Lasagna and baked ziti—American Italian food, so to speak—really wasn't our niche of food; he cooked really hearty stuff, using the heavy prosciuttos and the pastas and the smoked bacon and truffles. . . . By the time I was three or four, I was learning how to cook pasta with white truffles. He was a hard worker himself, and he wanted my sister, Nicoletta, and me to have a work ethic. We used to break the pasta in half and stir the butter or the sauce. We were always in the kitchen;

Thanksgiving we would have thirty people for a sit-down dinner. So the kitchen and learning how to cook and be a part of that whole aspect of entertaining was like the blood in our veins.

We used to have tutors, but there was a point where we went to school, and I remember coming home and he would be playing the piano and friends would be over. He made his debut at Carnegie Hall, playing piano, and he could sing opera; he had a beautiful voice. On weekends, we would go to Connecticut, to our country house in Greenwich—it was a beautiful home, roughly twenty-five thousand square feet on about nine acres directly on the water—and it was always filled with people. If we came home from school and my father wanted to go to Italy, we would literally pack up that afternoon and go off to the airport and have the whole staff come with us. It was a very exciting childhood we had, growing up with him.

Our family originated in Lucca around 1447, but they went to Florence in the late 1700s, and the family's had a home there since then. It's a truly amazing villa, and he loved to go there. My father's heart was always in Florence, my mother says, because we have the olive trees there, and the vineyards. Being in Florence energized him to come back to New York. We'd stay a minimum of a month; we had traveling tutors who would come over with us, so schooling was never an issue. We had these huge steamer trunks filled with clothes and food, and my father made sure that my sister and I always had things that reminded us of home. We would have men in these flatbed trucks pick us up. I have photos of the workmen on the back of the trucks taking off the trunks, and my sister and me in the courtyard opening them up and holding jars of peanut butter. It was always an adventure going places with my father.

He had us late in life. My mother was in her late thirties when she had us, and my father was in his late forties. He'd been married before and told that he wasn't going to be able to have children, so when he met my mother and they had us, it was like, "This was meant to be." Italians really have strong family values and ethics, so my father would never work from nine to five and then we'd see him for one hour, and then he'd have to go up to the office to do more work. For him, it was always "My family first and then my business." My aunt Mary, his sister, was the iron fist who ran the restaurant when my father would take these spontaneous trips or just want to relax with his family. "Brick House," they used to call her, because she put up with no nonsense. She did all the books, and my father trusted her wholeheartedly. And they had an enormous staff.

We were kidnapped at one point, when we were in France. My father always loved an entourage, so we would have our nannies with us, security, the whole thing. My mother and my sister and I and a nanny were in one car, and my father and his security were in another car, behind us. Our driver had set something up where my father's car broke down, and he just kept driving. We were taken to a kind of warehouse. You know, when you're kidnapped—it was a ransom kidnapping—it's usually for a couple of days. With my father, we were there for forty minutes. My father became Superman and rescued us.

Nothing happened to us and no ransom was given, and in forty minutes it was totally okay. I have no idea how he found us, but you didn't mess with his family. I think I was sixteen months old, but I've heard this story so many times, I feel like it happened yesterday.

The second time—I've been kidnapped twice—I was five or six. I was walking out of our building at 1165 Park Avenue, and I was put into a car. It had happened before; obviously my father had an awareness that it could happen again, so he had taught me, "No one can stand an annoying child. If it happens, you should do this kind of thing," and I did it. I was picking the leather off the headrests and being a total brat, kicking and screaming, and after literally five blocks, they were like, "Get him out of the car." My father also put us in karate classes when we were very young, so he knew that we could take care of ourselves.

We had a beautiful yacht, and we used to have quiet times when we'd go on the boat and unwind. When you're on a boat, you know, you'd have to either jump off and swim or have someone come and get you. It's interesting that his solace was in the middle of the ocean, where no one could touch us. And he loved cars. One vivid memory is driving with him; we had this huge stretch Cadillac with those wings, and I can remember sitting on his lap, holding that big steering wheel with the huge Cadillac emblem in front. He would have his hand underneath, but he was acting like I was steering, and the car was moving.

We had horses growing up, too, all these wonderful blessings. My father worked hard, and he definitely loved to play. He was just an amazing man. He always wanted us to be happy, and it was nice to have the material things, but having him there was the best thing, the most important thing. My father taught me that when I have children, whatever you're doing, you have to put them first. It's sad to see fathers who are not with their sons because of business—it's really, really sad because you don't know when you're going to die.

On the night of my seventh birthday, in 1987, he had a massive stroke. That evening he was playing the piano, singing "Happy Birthday" and all these songs, and I remember sitting with him. We had a pastry chef because of the restaurant, and my father had a birthday cake made with the image of whoever the superhero of that year was. I remember the cake coming, and sitting at the piano, and we went to bed, and that night we had to rush him to the hospital. My mother hoped that maybe he would pull through, so she kept him on the machine until he died about six days later. But technically, we lost him that night, and Delmonico's was closed soon after.

Who knows if he knew he was going to die so young? But it was almost as if he knew because he was always there for us, and because he enjoyed his life so much. He was so outgoing, creative, and spontaneous; he had such spirit. He was a character. I remember how he used to do a Charlie Chaplin kick, jumping up in the air and clicking his heels together. If I were to summarize him, it would be with the zest for life he showed in that Charlie Chaplin kick he had.

CRAIG NEWMARK

■

*Founder, chairman, and customer-service represen-
tative of Craigslist, www.craigslist.org, based in
San Francisco and serving fifty cities in the United
States, Canada, and England, attracting five mil-
lion visitors a month.*

MY FATHER, LEON NEWMARK, DIED when I was thirteen. We were living in Morristown, New Jersey. He was
a salesman for a meat-packing plant; at one time he sold promo-
tional items; he sold insurance. He was a heavy smoker and that's
why he died—at forty-three, I think, not long after I was bar
mitzvahed. Lung cancer.

I only have a few specific memories of him. I remember
playing catch with him a lot, and I remember him taking me to
a few Yankee games. We lived in northern Jersey, so the Yankees
were the home team. What I remember most distinctly was the
hot dogs—they had the cheap, steamed hot dogs—it was fun.
And I remember how he got us all on the roof of our garage a
couple of summers to see the fireworks nearby. I especially remember the time he saved my younger brother, Jeff, and me

from a nasty accident. We were alone in our station wagon, parked near our house on a little bit of a slope. I don't know what happened, I think the transmission slipped, and we started rolling. My dad was just about in the door of the house, and he jumped in the car and put the brake on. It seemed pretty heroic.

And I remember him seeing me get interested in girls. We were at a kind of low-rent pool club, and he was standing by the pool overlooking the shuffleboard courts, and I was playing shuffleboard with my kind-of girlfriend. At one point, I caught a glimpse of him watching, and I recall that he looked both pleased and mildly amused. I felt a little embarrassed.

I think losing my dad when I was so young made me—not tougher, but more independent, less emotionally dependent than most. I'm fine by myself. But I also think it took me much longer to learn people skills. I was already interested in the nerdy things, like math and science; I'm afraid that came much too naturally to me, plus I had a tendency to be introverted. Losing my dad perhaps warped me a bit further, but I've no idea about the way it did. I'm not quite certain how to articulate it, but there are some things I had to learn on my own where I could have used some help, like getting along with people better. I would have liked to have known that I shouldn't show off so much in class. (In my case, it wasn't in the class-clown way; it was in the knowing-all-the-answers way.) Being a show-off is the perfect way to alienate one's classmates, but I had to figure that out for myself.

I was the first in my family to go to college, and he would

have liked that. And I think he would have been very pleased with Craigslist, both in terms of what we do and the recognition we get for it. Craigslist is a place on the Net where you can address everyday needs, like finding a place to live or a job, maybe selling your stuff, or getting a date. I feel that one of the best things a person can do for another is to create a job. Nerd values are simple. It's good to make a good living. It's good to do well for your staff. You do okay commercially, and then you try to make a difference of some sort.

I don't remember enough of my upbringing to know how my dad would feel about that. I do know that some of my friends and family think I'm nuts for not having sold the business long ago and taken a lot of money for it. I like to think that my dad would understand, that he would get it, and get me. I think he'd probably be pleased and, probably, amused. I think of him as a guy who was pretty amused by life.

SUSAN LUCCI

Acclaimed talent of the screen and the stage, winning an Emmy Award for her role on All My Children. *She is a 2005 recipient of a star on the Hollywood Walk of Fame and also a successful entrepreneur.*

MY DAD GAVE ME A TREMENDOUS amount of love and attention. He was a hardworking man—he worked in the construction business—but when he was home, he spent a lot of time with me. He was a devoted father. He was also a very good artist and very creative. I think he had wanted to be an artist and couldn't pursue it. When I was little, he taught me how to draw and work with pastels and charcoal. We would sing together, and he would always read *The Night Before Christmas* with me.

My dad grew up during the Depression, and he didn't have the opportunities I had. For instance, there was no piano. When I took piano lessons, he saw that my interest was waning, so he took piano lessons, too, hoping to keep me involved. He took me for horseback-riding lessons, for ice-skating lessons—this was the greatest dad a girl could have.

One of my fondest memories is of being with my dad after a storm or a hurricane when I was seven or eight years old. We lived in a suburb of New York City, and he was always the first one in the community to go out and see if he could help. He'd look to see if any trees had fallen or if anyone was injured. And he always took me with him—not my older brother but me. I got to sit in the front seat with him and, well, it was very meaningful to me. My father would help a friend put in a concrete patio or do construction in his or her home. He would give someone the shirt off his back—and he did these things not to be noticed but because he could, and it was the right thing to do.

My father was first-generation Italian American, and during the time I was growing up, you might have expected him to emphasize education more for a boy than for a girl. But he didn't; he thought a good education was primary, and I grew up in a community where 98 or 99 percent of the students went on to college.

That was important to him. When I was a little girl, he used to introduce me to people as "Susan, the brains of the family, and she can do anything she puts her mind to." He gave me great confidence.

This was good because I was very shy. My mother always wanted me to go out and play with other kids. One sunny day when I was probably four, she locked me out of the house. I was banging on the screen door to come in, and my grandmother, who was living with us, told my mother she couldn't do this. My mother said, "She has to play with the other children." So

I did, but then I would go home and play by myself; I would make up stories and act out all the parts. My parents would hear me and think, "Oh, good, she made friends; some kids from the neighborhood are up there." But it was just me.

My parents were there for my first play, *Cindy Ellen*, which was based on *Cinderella*. I was a cheerleader in high school, and they were at every football game, every basketball game—they were my greatest cheerleaders. But my father wasn't so excited when I first said that I wanted to become an actress. There was no one in my family who was in the business. He was concerned that I was choosing something where there was a lot of rejection, a lot of criticism, and possibly a really hard life. He was also worried because I hadn't really been to the city except for trips with them to a Broadway play or Radio City Music Hall, and I had no sense of direction.

Also, I grew up in a town where everybody was very friendly, and he was afraid I would talk to strangers. He was street-smart, and he knew that I was not. But my parents had always encouraged me, and they let me try. My father always made me feel that I could do anything I wanted to do.

Fortunately, I started working right away. They were very proud and continued to be in the audience, watching me on TV. My mother still watches *All My Children* every day.

Erica Kane's father was a monster. He left when she was nine years old. He did some terrible things, and Erica has a lot of issues because of that—I don't know how I go there in my imagination. It's a little like the clown in the rodeo; you have to know how to ride really well before you can do the tricks. Maybe it's because my dad was so terrific with me that I can imagine what the absence of all that would be like.

My dad was still alive when I won the Emmy, and watching it on TV, he stood up in the living room and cheered. Before that, when I didn't win, he threatened to throw stuff at the screen. He died a year and a half ago. A lot of people said to my mother, "At least you had him all that time." And that's true, but the other side of the coin is that she lost her life partner. I miss him.

From my parents, I learned to always be there for my children. I made sure I was up in the morning to make their lunches and pack them off for school, and when I wasn't working, I was the one to pick them up from school. I always tried to schedule things so that I could protect my free time with them. And I was in the audience for each of the things they did. My son took karate lessons, and he played three sports at once at one point in his life; I would go to his practices and ball games and karate lessons and matches. When he began playing golf on the junior tour, my husband traveled with him as his personal valet and dad. It warmed my heart because, like my mother, I had also married a man who was a fabulous father.

GARY ERICKSON

◼

Founder and owner (with his wife, Kit) of Clif Bar, Inc., in Berkeley, California. In 2004 Reader's Digest named it the best mom-and-pop business in the country. Erickson is also the author, with Lois Lorentzen, of Raising the Bar: Integrity and Passion in Life and Business: The Story of Clif Bar, Inc.

WHEN I WAS IN FIFTH grade, my dad gave me his cornet, and that's when music became a big part of my life. I played trumpet in the junior high band, and in high school I started to play in jazz groups. My dad didn't have a problem with my pursuing jazz as a career if that's the direction I wanted to go. In fact, I started college as a music major, but I just couldn't see life as a horn player: clubs and smoke and drinks and being on the road. My dad also loved going to the mountains and skiing and fishing and hiking, and that became my thing, too. So I had these two pulls, one toward the city and the other into the mountains, and my dad introduced me to both.

I grew up in the middle, in the San Francisco Bay Area suburbs. My first memories of wilderness are of going to Yosemite as a family. We would drive through a blizzard to get to the mountains to ski at Badger Pass, my dad, my mom, and the three boys. This is back in the fifties and sixties; we had a big Pontiac with chains on the back. I remember the chain-control guys saying, "You can't go up there." And my dad saying, "I'm from Wisconsin; I know how to drive in the snow." "Okay, you can go."

Skiing wasn't as popular as it is today. It was a lot more dangerous because all the equipment was so archaic—wood skis and bear-trap bindings—sometimes when you fell, you wouldn't come out of your bindings. We're in the mountains, we're in blizzards, we're skiing in powder—my dad was willing to take the risk that people get hurt now and then. His passion rubbed off on me. My tolerance for risk is a little higher because of those early days of skiing, learning that if you get cold and wet, you're not going to die; if something breaks in your equipment, you can figure out how to fix it, even if you're in the mountains. It was all by example while doing it with him. Today my dad is seventy-nine, and he's an avid gardener. He has a big garden and he lives on a real steep hill, which he runs up and down all day. I call it extreme gardening.

One time we were at Incline Village, in Tahoe, and my cousin Kathleen got badly hurt skiing. My mom was freaking out because I'm ten years old and I want to go down the hardest, steepest slope, or black diamond, on the mountain, on these old skis. I wasn't that great a skier, and it was scary, but rather than saying, "You're right, Mary; we don't want him getting hurt," my dad said, "Let him do it. He can do it." I did the same thing with my daughter last year. I took her down a double black diamond in the Sierra, a ten-foot-wide chute of snow with rocks on both sides. She was super-scared, and I said, "Lydia, I know you can do it. You're a great skier, and I'll be right behind you." She was ten, too. She was so proud when she finished, she thanked me for encouraging her. Just like with my dad. I never would have skied down that mountain if he hadn't said, "You can do it."

Later, I got into rock climbing and mountaineering. People want things to be so clear and black-and-white and *easy* now. But in those sports, there's always a time when you don't have it all figured out, and the risk jumps up two or three notches, and you've got to work through it. Which I think applies to business, too.

I honored my father, Clifford Erickson, by naming my product after him when I developed a line of energy bars. I wanted something tough and strong like PowerBar, and I toyed with names like *Forza*, the Italian word for strength. But at the last minute, my father's name popped into my head. I wasn't thinking of a mountain cliff. I was thinking of how my dad introduced me to the wilderness, to the love of adventure and being independent and free.

DONALD J. TRUMP

Chairman and president of The Trump Organization; coproducer of The Apprentice, *on NBC.*

M Y FATHER, FRED C. TRUMP, was very disciplined but also very kind, and I think that's something everyone would say about him. He was a very solid person and citizen. As a father, he was the absolute best.

I remember him reading a lot, but what I recall most vividly is when he would take me along to his construction sites. That was incredibly exciting to me. To this day, I still enjoy visiting my sites through all the levels of development. My father never had to instill this interest in me—it was there. I was enthralled with construction and buildings from the beginning and I was fortunate that my father was in the industry. He had an enormous influence over me as an example to live up to. I continue to live by his high standards of professionalism.

The most important lesson I learned from my father was to

be responsible. He was a thoroughly responsible person. There aren't too many people like that, I've discovered. He set an example, without being self-righteous, that could challenge anyone. I couldn't have had a better example.

He had good advice, he was always on my side, and he was proud of me. I wish he could see how things have turned out with me, how terrific his grandchildren are, how lovely my fiancée Melania is, and share in my accomplishments. He meant so much to me, and the loss will always be there. I think of him every single day without fail.

Now, I expect my kids to do their best. I'm very lucky with the kids I have, because they all do their best and have respect for education. They are aware of their good fortune, just as I was.

GAYLE KING

Three-time Emmy Award–winning TV broadcaster, Editor at Large at O, The Oprah Magazine *and* O at Home, *and mother of two children, Kirby, a freshman at Stanford University, and William, a senior in high school.*

MY FATHER, SCOTT KING, WAS an electronic engineer. When I was in high school, the family moved from California to Chevy Chase, Maryland, but I stayed behind and lived with my geography teacher and his wife so that I could finish my senior year. Right before graduation, my dad wrote me an unbelievable letter, saying how proud he was of me for starting this new phase of my life, and that he knew that I could do and be *anything* that I wanted to be. I was so excited to get that letter because he was the first person to verbalize that idea to me. How empowering it was to a young girl to know that: "Wow, I can?" I thought. It is thrilling and comforting to know that somebody totally, totally believes in you.

I think a girl who doesn't have a good relationship with her father has such a disadvantage in life, because fathers can give you such self-esteem, such confidence in yourself. As you make your way in the world, it's good to know that, from a male standpoint, there's someone who cares about you and thinks that you are the greatest, most beautiful thing. That will take you a long way. The voices in the outside world get so nasty sometimes, but when you have that kind of foundation, you don't have to buy into any of the negativity out there, because you have somebody who bolsters and supports you. It's so key. That's why so many girls get into trouble. They're looking for love—here's a cliché—in all the wrong places. They're trying to fill a hole.

Even today, when fathers are more actively involved in their kids' lives, most of them don't know the sizes of the kids' clothes, or their teachers' names, or the kids' schedules; most of them don't know when they need to go to the dentist or have a checkup. That's still left to the women in most houses; that's just how it works. But a father gives you things that a mother can't. I see in my own house—I have a son and a daughter—that you have a special bond with your dad that you don't have with your mother. It's equally important, but different.

That letter meant even more to me coming from a man who was not physically demonstrative. It didn't bother me, because I didn't know any other way. With my own children, I am very affectionate. I now think that's so important, and I ask myself, "How did I know I was loved when we didn't get a lot of hugs and kisses?" But I just knew it. I knew that I was loved and protected. He would read to us, and he would drive and take us places and do things with us, but he wasn't a touchy-feely kind of guy. Looking back at his life, he didn't come from a dad who was very demonstrative, either. It's so true: You really do learn what you see. So to get that letter, where he said how much he loved and cared about me and how far I could go in life—it was like, "WOW."

When I think of him from my little-girl vantage point, I think, "He's so big and tall." Now I realize that he was five feet eleven and his weight was 170; that's not so huge. But I thought he was so tall and big and strong, and that he could do *anything.* There was no situation my father couldn't handle, no word he didn't know. I can remember asking, "What does *barrister* mean?" and thinking, "He knows big words." There was nothing I could ask him that he wouldn't know the answer to.

My father was a very strict disciplinarian in terms of grades: Cs were not acceptable in my house. If you came home from school and didn't have any homework, he would ask you a couple of questions, which I remember to this day. I remember telling him that six times six was thirty-two. And him saying, "See? You don't know," and I had to sit there and do the multiplication tables. He would come up with homework for you to do if you didn't bring any home.

I am amazed at the awe I felt of him, and at my feeling that you could never second-guess or challenge him. I think you ought to be able to feel that you can challenge your parents without being disrespectful. I am the oldest of four girls, but I was the only one that tried that tactic.

He died when I was eighteen, just as we were getting into the friendship phase of our relationship. Up until that point, it had been parent and child, very much so. I can remember that first year I went to college, inviting a guy home for Thanksgiving, and my father was so resistant. He was very verbal about how he didn't think it was good idea to bring a young man I'd just met home. I remember saying, "You're wrong; you haven't even met him. And besides that, Daddy, he's not a boyfriend; he's just a friend. I was just trying to be nice because he doesn't have anywhere to go." And when my friend came, my father was so nice, so kind, and so welcoming. I thought, "Who is this guy, who was acting so ugly yesterday about somebody coming?" Later I learned that he told my mother, "I really have to hand it to Jeepy"—he called me Jeepy because my full name is Gayle Patrice (G.P.)—"I got the biggest kick when she was standing up to me." So it seems he was starting to enjoy the fact that I would challenge him and say, "You know, what you are saying just doesn't make any sense to me."

I feel very sad that he never saw any of my children or met my husband. He never saw the key milestones in my life: my marriage, my children, my first job—my divorce. My ex-father-in-law is also dead, and just the other day my daughter said to me, "Gosh, I've never had a grandfather." I had been without my father for so long I'd never thought of her having a sense of loss. One of my biggest regrets is that he never got a chance to see me on the news. We used to have to watch the news as a family every night. Walter Cronkite was our anchor of choice.

My father said, "You should always know what's going on in the world, and the news changes every day." He would have gotten such a kick out of seeing me because he was such a news junkie. The first time I anchored the news, I so wished he could see that I'd ended up in television after complaining so often, "We have to watch the *news*? Why?" I remember thinking, "Boy, I wish he could see this. Scott King would be very proud."

ANDREW CUOMO

Founder in 1986 of New York's Housing Enterprise for the Less Privileged (H.E.L.P.), which became the nation's largest private provider of transitional housing for the homeless; Secretary of Housing and Urban Development, 1997–2001; head of the New York City Commission on the Homeless, 1991; Assistant District Attorney in Manhattan, 1984 and 1985; ran for governor of New York, 2002; author and editor of Crossroads: The Future of American Politics, *published by Random House in 2004.*

I GREW UP IN QUEENS, NEW YORK. My father, Mario Cuomo, was born and raised in Queens, and we stayed there until he became governor and moved to Albany in 1982. All through my childhood, he was a practicing lawyer in a Brooklyn firm. At that time, the most prestigious law firms were in Manhattan. Many ethnic law students—Italians, Jews—couldn't get into the so-called Manhattan white-shoe firms and therefore went to Brooklyn firms. This was all much more accepted then; discrimination was not as readily actionable and diversity was not as valued. There was much more reliance on connections and legacy.

I was raised in a Democratic city, Democratic state, and Democratic family. Democrats were focused on the progress of lower-class and working people, people who were not of the powerful and the placed. Democratic policies were those that would help people who relied on public institutions for education, health care, and so on. That was very much our culture. And my father had a penchant for pro bono cases and community activism. In one case, the city was condemning sixty-nine homes in Corona, a working-class area of Queens, in order to put in a ball field for a high school. He represented the homeowners against the city, and most of the homes were saved. It was essentially a pro bono case because the residents were all poor and could not pay for his services.

My father was busy, he was working, but he was always accessible and supportive and a lot of fun. As a dad, he was great. He was very athletic, and we played a lot of basketball and baseball together. Sunday was a big family day when we were kids. Our family lived a couple of blocks from my father's parents, in Queens, and my mother's parents were from Brooklyn, which was always a nice Sunday ride. Every Sunday we would go back and forth to see our grandparents—sometimes to Queens, sometimes to Brooklyn. You'd eat for twenty-three consecutive hours and then nap. The grown-ups would debate the issues of the day around the table, and the kids would go play ball in the street. It was a very simple, uncomplicated lifestyle.

But then my father ran for office, and I got involved in politics with him. First he ran for mayor in 1977. I was going to Fordham University, and I basically became the campaign manager for the Bronx. He lost that race to a fellow named Ed Koch. The following year, he ran for lieutenant governor, and I was his deputy campaign manager. When Koch ran for governor of New York in 1982 and my father challenged him, I became his campaign manager. He was a phenomenal long shot because Koch was a national figure and was thought to be unbeatable. That was a very, very difficult race, but my father won a surprise upset.

After that, I was always involved in my father's political life, even in the off years, and it added another dimension to the relationship. It's different than running a shoe store together as a father and son. In many ways, it's live or die on a campaign. We used to say kiddingly, "Either we'll never talk again after this, or we will be closer than ever." In our case, it served to bring us closer, and to know each other on a level that most fathers and sons don't have the opportunity to share.

Being his campaign manager was formative for us. In a campaign, you didn't just see him as a father anymore, around the dinner table or on a ball field. I was literally with him twenty-four hours a day, seven days a week, for years. So just in terms of time, you get to know each other better. And in terms of your interactions—it's not just personal anymore, it's the most profound and most intimate professional interaction. You get to see the strengths and the weaknesses of the man; you see how the personal interacts with the professional.

What my father showed me during the political campaigns—which I've appreciated more, frankly, as I've gotten older—is that politics is about principle; that's what the entire effort is about. My father is a very liberal, progressive person. He believes that the private market is not perfect, and if you leave the market to its own devices, many people will be left out and left behind. You need government—efficient, effective government—to make the playing field fair and to help people lift themselves up. That is an important and legitimate social pursuit. A political campaign is a crusade for an ideology and a set of beliefs—which you then implement through government, through programs. It is about a different set of values, with a different end in sight. And that's what justifies the entire enterprise.

For example, when my father was running for office, the death penalty was one of the most powerful issues in the state. In 1977 it was the summer of Son of Sam, a serial killer in New York, and people were petrified. Eighty percent of them wanted to put the death penalty on the books. My father was against the death penalty. When he ran for governor, the pollsters all told him, "You cannot win with this position. You must change your position on this; it's the one issue that everyone cares about, and eighty percent of them are against you." However, he refused to change his position. And he won despite it, which none of the pundits believed was possible. People concluded, in a way that no poll could ever calculate, "What's more important to me is to have a guy I respect, and I respect him for having the courage to disagree with me."

You could argue that the flip side of adherence to your principles is inflexibility. That's true almost by definition. I don't find that a shortcoming; I find it something admirable. You do have to be discerning in your selection of principle. Governance is the art of compromise, but there's a definite balance between compromising and forsaking.

When my father lost his race for reelection as governor in 1994, he had a grace in defeat that was powerful to me. It was not just that he was gracious in a public statement, he truly was at peace. It gets back to point one: You fight the good fight, and winning or losing is less important than making the case for what you believe. My father had honored the principle of the good fight, and that gave him peace.

My father is a fundamentally grounded person. He's very good at keeping his eye on the ball and keeping his foundation strong. He doesn't need fame or fortune to validate his existence. He believes in public service in the fullest meaning of the word: *service*. I remember him saying to me at that time, "The same friends we had at the beginning of the business are the friends we'll have at the end of the business, and if they're not our friends because we lost, then they were never our friends anyway." My father was not in politics for the pursuit of staying in politics. I think if you asked him, he would say, "I'd rather lose defending principle than win forsaking principle." That is a powerful example that I've kept with me.

When I was a kid and the Corona homeowners would come over to our house, it was clear that they were reliant on my father, and so appreciative for all he did. Those visits gave me the sense that he was a hero. I thought, "Look at him. My dad is fighting all the dragons, the powerful dragons that are trying to hurt these poor people."

ASHLEIGH BANFIELD

*Emmy Award–winning international TV
correspondent and host.*

E VERYONE THINKS HIS OR HER DAD is the greatest. There
are T-shirts that tell you so. It's a phrase often repeated
early in life—"My dad is the greatest"—only to be muted or
forgotten, sometimes for decades. But there is really nobody
who compares to a dad.

My dad is eighty. John Alexander Banfield hit that mile-
marker on May 24, 2004. Yowza! I think my three siblings and
I, each in our respective corners of North America, did a collec-
tive shoulder-drop, staring off above our computer screens and
doing the philosophical math. Eighty. Jeez Louise! That's five
sweet sixteens, six global wars, eight distinct fashion eras, seven
grandchildren, and most important, more than one whole me! It
certainly adds up to an awful lot of hassle to survive. No wonder he gets a little grumpy now and then. No wonder he forgets

a few things (albeit fewer than I do). There must be loads of data damming up his emotional pools and memory banks. If it were me, I'd need a prescription just to say hello.

The whole idea of Dad turning eighty would be easier to digest if he looked anywhere near his age. Here's a guy who smoked a lot (when smokers still displayed their fresh cigarettes in pretty silver dishes), who has rarely exercised (yet could always beat Mum in tennis), and who has eaten everything on the horizon (with a particular penchant for lipids and trans fat). That said, he is still far from the vision of health. He's had a hip replaced, had dizzy spells, and made many a late-night phone call to his doctor. (Sample transcript from Dad's end: "Yeah . . . ? Ya think . . . ? Oh, for Pete's sake!")

Still, friends who've known him all his life always marvel at his age, and how young he seems.

I like to think it's because of the hobbies he keeps. We're told that hobbies are good for you, that they keep your mind challenged and focused, that they make your "happy-pores" tingle, and that they keep you reaching for the phone to update everyone with news of your discoveries.

Dad is pretty busy with his hobbies. They occupy his entire day. I figured it would be a tough transition for someone who was used to being a busy architect and builder in Winnipeg, Canada, all his life. But now, it's nine-to-five hobbies! And apparently, it was not such a tough switch for Dad!

He's constantly clipping ideas, making notes, drawing designs, and sending them off to all the important people in his life. And he never misses a deadline.

Imagine being so dedicated to your hobbies that you would put as much energy into them as you did into your professional workday. My siblings and I always wonder . . . what kind of hobbies could intrigue Dad so deeply that he's committed every waking hour to them? What kind of hobbies have him so committed that giving them his constant focus and energy is, in turn, keeping him young and vibrant? What kind of hobbies can elicit a grin, proud and wide, every time he shares the fruits of his efforts?

Turns out my father's hobbies are . . . keeping tabs on my brothers, my sister, and me.

PETER GREENBERG

■

Travel editor of NBC's Today *show, author of* The Travel Detective *series (Villard), and chief correspondent for the Discovery Network's Travel Channel.*

S IDNEY GREENBERG WALKED. HE DIDN'T run. He listened. He never yelled.

As a child in New York, afflicted with ileitis, an insidious disease of the intestine that he wasn't supposed to survive, my father never learned how to ride a bicycle, swim, or throw a baseball, and so he couldn't teach me. But now I know how much I learned from him.

A dedicated physician, a brilliant pathologist and diagnostician, he was the embodiment of the Paul Muni character in *The Last Angry Man*. He was devoted to his patients, comforted them in their fears, and embraced their hopes. He was not a professional corporation. He simply and lovingly practiced internal medicine. And as I watched him do what he loved to do, he taught me about life.

His patients were devoted to him, too. My father believed that you couldn't care for your patients unless you cared about them. You couldn't treat them if you didn't hear them. His waiting room was always filled, almost overcrowded, with those who waited to see him and never complained. All his patients knew that when their time came to see "the Doctor," they'd get my father's undivided attention, for thirty minutes, an hour, longer.

As a very young child, I never saw much of my father because I was usually asleep by the time he came home from his office or his appointed rounds at the hospital. So I had to wait, too. About the time I turned ten, we started spending more time together. And it was worth the wait, because once a week, usually on a Saturday afternoon, we would leave our apartment building and take long walks, just the two of us, through the streets of the Upper East Side. We would always stop for lunch. Along the way, he talked about his patients and some of his cases, but what he was really doing was sharing the life-and-death morality stories of all our lives, relating their illnesses and ailments to my own young and naive sense of health, well-being, and fear of the unknown.

And the medical reports from my father always led to a discussion on his philosophy of life.

"Success is not about winning or losing," he told me on more than one occasion, when I felt I had been treated unfairly, or my team hadn't been victorious, or another kid in class had gotten a higher grade than I had. "It's not about having or not having. Or being right or wrong, good or bad, happy or sad. It's really quite simple. Your real success in life comes from adjusting," he'd say. "How well you adjust, how quickly you adjust, and how sensitively you adjust will make all the difference at the end of the day."

My father taught me to have a plan B and a plan C. He showed me that when plan C didn't work, I should never forget about D, E, and F. He taught me that it was much more important to be interested than interesting. To listen well. To act slowly after thinking something through. To be spontaneous, but not irresponsible. To take responsibility for the things I could control, not dwell on the things I couldn't.

When it came to finances, my father paid as he went. He had one credit card for emergency use only, and I never saw him use it. He wrote all his bills by hand. If his patients had the money, they paid. If not, well, they still needed to be helped. Lots of people owed my father when he died, in 1991. But he died owing no one.

The one thing my father didn't do was cheerlead. He was at the hospital or at the office when I played in my school softball games, and swam in my first race, and played in my first piano recital. When I was a junior in college and wrote bylined pieces for *Newsweek,* he never picked up the phone to congratulate me. He came from a generation where the son called the father, not vice versa. Every time I called, he said he'd been just about to call me, a ritual that was repeated almost every time I dialed his number. I always wondered if he read my stories, or, later, if he ever saw me on television.

It was only when he died that I received what I had been seeking from him all my life. It came when I least expected it—at his memorial service. I was approached by literally dozens of his patients, most of whom I had never met. Each proceeded to tell me in intimate detail about virtually every news or feature story I had ever written, every movie I had produced, every book I had written. My father never was a cheerleader with me, but he certainly had been a cheerleader for me. He had read it all, had seen it all, and had proudly told everyone he knew about me.

He just never could tell me.

But at that memorial service, it all came full circle. The closure was palpable. As each person came up to speak to me, it was really my father I was hearing, and I could hear his voice clearly, shouting my praises.

DEAN ORNISH, MD

Founder and president of the nonprofit Preventive Medicine and Research Institute, in Sausalito, California; clinical professor of medicine at the University of California, San Francisco. He directed research that demonstrated for the first time that diet and lifestyle changes may begin to reverse heart disease. Selected by LIFE *magazine as one of the "50 most influential members of his generation."*

ONE OF THE REASONS THAT my father, Dr. Edwin Ornish, who's almost eighty now, became a dentist was so that he could always be home for dinner and spend weekends with his family. He loved music and played the clarinet; he loved the jazz clarinet that Benny Goodman played. At one point he had even thought about being a musician, but he said, "I'm not going to do that because I'd be on the road all the time, and I wouldn't be with my family."

My father and I (and occasionally my uncle; later it was with my younger brother) would go watch the Dallas Cowboys play football at the Cotton Bowl, back when Don Meredith was the quarterback, and "Bullet" Bob Hayes was the fastest man alive, and Roger Staubach was the backup quarterback. We'd go fishing, we would go camping with the Boy Scouts, and my father taught me how to play baseball. He was left-handed, so he played first base, but I learned how to play all the positions.

In my work I have spent so much time with so many accomplished people, and their biggest regret is that they didn't spend time with their families. It's not even quality time or what you do, necessarily; it's just being there. My father would be there when I woke up in the morning and have breakfast with me, and he would be home most nights in time for dinner. If I ever needed him, he would leave the office early. I didn't fully appreciate at the time how rare and precious that is, and how much that affected my view of the world as a loving place rather than a hostile, dangerous place.

My natural inclination is to trust people until proven otherwise, because I come from a loving, trusting family. As opposed to so many people who say things like "Only the paranoid survive." Of course, you get hurt at times when you go around with an open heart, but if your heart is closed, it's much harder to connect with people. You can only be intimate to the degree that you can allow yourself to be vulnerable, and you can only be vulnerable to the degree that you feel that sense of trust. And trust, more than from any other single place, comes from the kind of relationship that you have with your parents. I understand that not everyone has the luxury of spending time with their kid to that degree—single parents have to work and put their kids in day care, and it's not about feeling guilty if you can't do it—but I honor and respect both my parents because their prime directive was to find careers that enabled them to spend the most time possible with their kids.

Study after study has shown that people who feel lonely and depressed and isolated are many times more likely to get sick and die prematurely. It's at least as important as smoking or diet, and it certainly plays a role in why people smoke or overeat or drink too much or work too hard or abuse substances of different kinds. Those are often ways of trying to numb or kill or distract themselves from the pain and loneliness that comes from not having had that family closeness early in life.

I became a father four years ago, and the time that I spend with my son, Lucas, and my wife, Molly, is so much better than just about anything else I could be doing. It's helped me appreciate even more what my father did. I do the best that I can to be there for my son. I'll read him a story and he'll go to sleep; then I'll take a red-eye to New York, have a morning meeting, come back to San Francisco that afternoon, and be there in time to have dinner with him the next night and put him to bed again.

The other thing I learned from my father that really influenced my life was the importance of prevention. He taught me that if you don't treat the underlying cause, more often than not the same problem comes back again. Or you get a new set of problems or side effects, or you have painful choices to make. He'd tell me, "I just don't understand my patients. I say, 'You have to brush your teeth,' and they'll say, 'Well, I'll just get false teeth when they fall out.'" I used to work in his office; because I was interested in photography, he would let me develop his X-rays, which also gave me a sense of responsibility. So I could see where the cavities were in the X-rays, and he'd say, "Most of these are preventable, if people were just willing to make different choices."

He was a pioneer in advocating fluoridation—and you know, in Dallas at the time, that took a lot of courage, with the John Birch Society and all the people who'd say, "You're a Communist if you're in favor of fluoridation." Preventing cavities was something that worked against his economic advantage, too, because a lot of a dentist's income comes from filling teeth. But he believed it was the right thing to do.

At one point I even thought of going to dental school and taking over my father's practice. He said he liked being a dentist because he was his own boss, and that way he could act with integrity without having to worry about his career. That's why he really wanted me to become a dentist. What he really was saying was, If it's not dentistry, do something that will give you the pleasure of serving other people in ways that make a meaningful impact on their lives, and that will also give you independence. When you can be your own boss, you can control your life; and when you control your life, you can make choices like spending time with your kids and doing what you think is right without having to worry that your family is going to suffer. I don't have to worry about that because I incorporated the values that I learned in this area from my father.

VIJAY SINGH

*PGA TOUR Player of the Year (2004); two-time
Arnold Palmer Award winner as the PGA TOUR's
leading money winner (2003–2004); winner of
more than 55 PGA TOUR and international tournaments. Vijay has been a member of the International Team in five Presidents Cups.*

WHEN I WAS GROWING UP in Fiji, golf was not one of the
sports that people played the way they do in America.
But I was very fortunate because my father, Mohan Singh, was a
very good golfer, and whenever he would buy new clubs, my
brothers and I would get his old ones. I had a full set of clubs by
the time I was twelve. That meant I could go out and play and
get much better than would have been possible if I had just had
one club.

My father played in Fiji, but golf was not his job. He was an
excellent airline technician, in charge of refueling the aircraft.
Golf started out as a sport for him but became more serious. He
competed at the club level; he was captain of the club. I caddied
for him for a long time, and that's where I learned to play.

Where I grew up, fathers were strict, and you respected the

dad more. You didn't speak to your father as much as children do in a Western society. It was a tense relationship as father and son. When I was growing up, you could say things to your dad, but you'd have to pick your time and place to say them. You didn't just say what was on your mind. It wasn't a bad thing. It's just the way life was, and we accepted it.

My father was a very fair man, but he was also a very strict person, and we were disciplined in a way that's lacking here. We weren't supposed to do anything out of line, and he kept us in line. We never complained. It was not necessarily correct, but you learn from those things and adjust.

For example, if I was hitting balls at the club where I wasn't supposed to, other guys would not say anything, but my dad would come up and say, "You can't do that." If I was playing a hole where others were playing and I just cut in, he would come and tell me straightaway, in a polite way, that I could not do that. The greatest gift he gave me was honesty. He was always very fair with rules, and he was the most honest guy on the course.

He lives in New Zealand now, and he's very proud of my success. I'm sure he talks about it more with his friends when I'm not around. He was here for the Masters this year, and we had a great, great time. It was the first time he had come to America, the first time he saw me play, and the second time he met my fourteen-year-old boy, Qass. It was wonderful. He came and stayed with me for a week and a half after the tournament. We all had dinners together and talked about little things here and there, in our way. He had a better relationship with my boy than he'd had with me. It was a way of getting closer to me.

I'm trying to have a better relationship with Qass than I had with my dad. You have to nudge but not force. I will sit down with him and try to talk with him about school and how he's doing and any problems he might have.

Qass and I played in a father-son tournament last year, and I think it was the biggest thrill I've ever had in my career—the best time I ever had on a golf course. It was the first activity I've ever done with him. I'm sure I enjoyed it far more than he did, but now he tells me he's looking forward to the next one as much as I am.

BOBBI BROWN

Founder and CEO, Bobbi Brown Cosmetics.

THERE IS NO ONE IN THE WORLD I love as much as my dad. It's a different love from the one I have for my husband and children. My dad, James Brown, is the closest person in the universe to me. He is the guy I called first when I'd had a bad day, when I sold my company, when I met the man I was going to marry. I mean, he is just right there!

At the ripe old age of forty-seven, I still need him to say, "Great job; good; you look great. . . ." I still need his approval after all these years, even after I've totally surpassed any expectations he might have had for me.

As a kid, I was in awe of him. My girlfriends nicknamed him "Gorge," because he was gorgeous and everybody was always in love with him. He was definitely the cool dad, no question. He was handsome; he rode a motorcycle; he was talented and successful. He didn't come from people who had money; I think his dad was a tailor. So he really made it himself, going to law school and becoming an attorney. Later he stopped being a lawyer, and he wrote travel pieces for a lifestyle magazine. He went from looking like Michael Landon to looking like Michael Douglas, or Kirk Douglas as he gets older.

He's incredibly smart and very creative. He used to sit with me with clay and paint, and he would take me into his darkroom when he was doing his black-and-white photography. I was not a good student, I was not the smart daughter. I was the creative, nice daughter, and I guess he realized early on that he was not going to fight that report-card battle, so we've had a good relationship most of our lives. It's very easy to want your child to be everything you weren't. What he instilled in me was to respect and be nice to people, to be creative, to find things I love, and to continually learn and better myself. This has really helped me.

My dad was the opposite of strict. He was the first one I told when I tried something bad when I was a kid. I came home and told him, and who does that? A lot of parents would never even discuss the subject of sex or drugs. But I remember, growing up, my dad and his friends downstairs on their way to a Crosby, Stills and Nash concert, or going somewhere else. My parents were twenty-one when I was born, so they were out doing fun things, and I was home with the babysitter.

There is absolutely no question that I'm a better mom because I've seen my father parent, and he's a much better grandfather than he was a father. He was the hip, cool dad I was in love with and in awe of, but he wasn't necessarily the doting father that I have now. And he is the most incredibly doting grandfather. He's come to visit from Chicago every other month since my fourteen-year-old was born. Every picture in my photo album is of my dad and us doing something together. He's been a huge part of my kids' lives. I don't think he's making up for anything, because I don't think he feels bad about it; he just accepts what was. I'm very much that way, too. I don't feel bad about the past. I just deal with what needs to be dealt with now. I don't hold any regrets or feel pained because my dad wasn't the nurturing, perfect father that I know my husband is to his kids.

In other ways, my husband is a lot like my dad: smart, well-read, opinionated, fun. And they are incredibly close. Sometimes when I haven't talked to my dad all week, I'll call him up and say, "Hey, where have you been?" And he'll say, "I've talked to Steve three or four times." One of the best things my dad ever taught me was how absolutely ridiculous it is to ever be mad at my husband. You know, in life and in marriage, no matter what, you've got to be able to say, "I'm sorry I upset you," and to put your husband first and be close. It works in my marriage. My dad has also taught me how to compartmentalize my day-to-day things, because I can get overwhelmed, and that has helped immensely.

He is turning seventy soon, and he is in the best shape of his life. He plays racquetball; he does weight-training; he eats healthy food; he travels the world; and he's very happy in his marriage.

He's a wonderful role model for me, and the thought that one day he won't be here—well, I try not to go there. But I have said everything to my dad. I tell him when I'm upset; I tell him I love him; and I tell him how much he means to me. That's my biggest advice for any human being: Never hold back what's on your mind. I'm really lucky because he's my father and my friend.

MARIA BARTIROMO

■

Host of NBC's syndicated half-hour weekly program
The Wall Street Journal Report with Maria Bartiromo, *plus two weekday business-news programs
on CNBC. Bartiromo was the first journalist to
report live from the floor of the New York Stock Exchange on a daily basis. She has a regular column in*
Reader's Digest *and is the author of* Use the News:
How to Separate the Noise from the Investment
Nuggets and Make Money in Any Economy.

MY FATHER, VINCENT BARTIROMO, WAS not an economics guy, but he owned a restaurant, the Rex Manor,
in Brooklyn. We had two rooms for catering weddings and private parties, a big restaurant, a big bar area, a pizza oven. . . . It
was very much a family business, but to me it was big business,
and I particularly remember going there on Mondays with my
father and watching him do the books. While the restaurant was
bustling up front, he and his partner would sit in the back, in
one of the dining rooms—on Mondays we were closed for
weddings—and do the books together. I can't say I knew exactly
what was going on, but I would always see him there, with his

big calculator and all the books spread out, going through revenue and earnings, and that was a major influence on me. Years later, I recognized that it was my father who had sort of planted the seeds in my head of taking ownership of something and of wanting to pursue a business career.

My grandfather opened the restaurant more than fifty years ago. I would walk into the kitchen and see him sitting in the corner of the room overseeing everything, and when my grandfather passed away, my father took it over. On Tuesdays, he'd be in the kitchen sweating; he was very much an operations guy, and he'd be making sure that everybody was doing what they needed to be doing.

My father is very down-to-earth, very humble, very easygoing, and that's why he has the greatest demeanor. He's easy to get along with; he doesn't allow anything to bother him. The biggest influence I've had from my father is watching him work so hard. Even though he doesn't come across as stressed-out, he gets everything done. And he's also very generous. He would have a long day at work, and then he would bring pizza pies home for the whole block. Everyone on the block loved my father.

At home he cooked all the time. Because he owned the restaurant, he would always cook for an army, and my mom would say, "I hate when you cook because you leave my kitchen a mess," because he was always using all these pans and cooking for so many people when it was just us, my parents and three kids.

And because the restaurant business is so demanding, it

forced all of us to be there together; otherwise we wouldn't see each other. On holidays, I became the coat-check girl; my sister was a hostess; my brother was a waiter. And so I learned a lot of lessons about teamwork, and about how supportive a family can be.

My father encouraged me to work hard, do the right thing, love what you do—but the only way you can work really hard is if you really love what you do. He encouraged me not in a direct or specific way, just in the way he approached his life, and the way he approached his work. Now he watches my shows all the time, and he wears his CNBC hat all the time—he's very proud. My parents are both so proud and loving, and we have such a strong and close-knit family. That goes a long way in an up-bringing, when you feel your problems are your family's problems, and know your family has such love and support for you. It really gives a person confidence.

JON STEWART

■

Host of the Emmy and Peabody Award–winning The Daily Show with Jon Stewart *and co-author of the* New York Times *#1 best-selling* America (The Book).

IT'S THE MOST INSANE, SURREAL thing, the moment your son is born. It became clear to me immediately, when my son was born in the summer of 2004, that I could kill if anything was going to happen to him. If somebody wasn't putting the thermostat on the right temperature there in the hospital, I could kill that person. It's a strange, new feeling of wanting to protect this young man at all costs.

My wife and I found out the sex of the baby early on, and we had a name early on. We had been talking to him and using his name, so in some respects I felt I already knew him. There was just a sense of "Hey, when are you going to come out to play?" We always knew that it was Nathan; it was just a question of meeting him.

So far, fatherhood is great. Women, I think, face more

disappointment than men about their children because their expectations are higher. I just hope that when I look at Nathan, he
doesn't cry. In that sense, I've already achieved my goal. So the key
to fatherhood is low expectations: "Wow, he called me once this
year; he must love me a lot."

I remember when I won an Emmy wanting to hold the tro-
phy up right at the camera, because Nate had stayed home with
my wife, and say, "You see, showbiz is important, too. That's why
I had to leave, don't you get it?" I'm looking to work it this way:
to being so ineffectual a father as to not be needed. That would
remove the dilemma of having to travel. My son will say, "Oh,
you're leaving for a week? Okay, see you Monday."

Actually, getting a job that I went to every day is what
grounded my life enough to be able to get married and start having a family and all that. Being on the road all the time is no way
to begin things. I know I would have worried about it when I
was still drinking and smoking. Now that I'm older, I know that
he will be okay financially. And I'm not torn, thinking, "Gee,
everybody is going out to the bar tonight, and they are all watching the game. That's over for me." I'm not pulled in that direction
because my wife and I are such homebodies, we always joked
that we would be the first people who, after having a kid, would
go out *more*.

I think what I'm looking forward to most as he grows up is
seeing his interpretation of things. I'm bored with myself, so the
idea that this new guy is coming in, with a whole new way of
looking at things, that's exciting.

I don't know that I will ever be ready for all the craziness that comes in New York with trying to get into the best preschool and elementary school and all that. The idea of getting them up on the treadmill and having them run as fast as they can for as long as they can because anything else will diminish their chances of having a happy, healthy life—I don't buy that. I think we may just homeschool. We might just try and create the "bubble." Make sure the diner delivers and brings in textbooks, too.

I don't feel I've made the leap yet to the general notion that "Everybody is somebody's child." For me, it's still "How will this affect my child?" It's a more selfish, less altruistic thought process; maybe that will change. My wife has already said that sometimes she'll be walking on the street and start thinking, "Each of these people is someone's child. All of these people once were looked at in the way that we look at our child; somebody once felt he or she would do anything to help this person." It's so interesting now to see people who are down on their luck or having a rough time of it, and to realize that person's situation is tearing the heart out of some people somewhere. It's the way you begin to connect with the rest of the world. Maybe it's that sense of something larger than yourself, which to people in showbiz is anathema.

Wearing a seat belt and stopping smoking made me feel I was doing pretty much all that I could do for myself. But now you've got this other person, and you want to make sure that he's okay. It's a fear that I've never felt before, and such happiness at the same time.

KELLY RIPA

Co-host of Live with Regis and Kelly *and star of ABC's* Hope & Faith.

MY DAD TOLD ME AT an early age that as long as I was willing to work hard I could do anything I want, anything I set my mind to. I decided I wanted to go to New York and make my way as an actress. I knew I was disappointing him because he really wanted me to go to college, but once he saw how strong my desire was, he was completely encouraging. He would drive me to auditions, or lend me the busfare to get there.

In our family, it was all about the work. You had to work; no matter what you were doing, no matter what it was that you wanted to do, you better work for it and you better earn your way. His entire life was an example of that, and when you have that kind of example, you can't go wrong. Even now, his favorite piece of advice, his catchphrase, is "Keep your nose to the grindstone, sweetheart." When my husband, Mark, and I go home to visit my parents, to this day, he'll put us both to work—weeding the garden, scrubbing the trashcan, something like that, reminding me not to get "too big for my britches."

My dad was a bus driver for the New Jersey Transit Authority for twenty-five years and worked tirelessly, endlessly. It was a huge treat for us when he would take us to the depot and let us get on the bus. It was magical. He seemed so powerful. He wasn't a big man, but when I was little he seemed huge—like he was the largest man on the planet. To me he had the most important job in the world.

Usually he got home after we had all gone to bed. He did it all so that my mom didn't have to work and so that we could have piano lessons and ballet classes and all the little extra things. In fact, one of my earliest memories of him is that he bought me a book, a *Sesame Street* book, when my sister was born. I think he just wanted me to feel important and special. And even though he woke up at 4 a.m. to go to work and never turned down overtime, on the weekends he made it his mission to get up extra early and take us to the Jersey Shore or the zoo, or just do amazing things with us because he wanted his moments with us to count.

Even though he was working, his presence was felt at all times—in fact, if one of us woke up in the middle of the night with a fever or from a nightmare, we always called for Dad. He was the one who would get up and come into our room. Usually, he'd just be getting off work anyway, but he was our great protector. I always felt safe when my dad was around.

I know I married Mark because he reminded me of my father. They both have that strong work ethic, and both are very involved, sensitive parents. I remember when my grandparents died, my father was the one who told us and he cried. That was an important thing—that men could cry and that it was okay. Mark is the kind of guy who will fly home from a business trip just to go to a parent/teacher meeting and then go right back to work.

My dad was the most sophisticated, elegant man I had ever known. He was chivalrous and a gentleman—in fact, early on in my career, I always brought him to the Emmys as my date. When I met Mark, he was the only man other than my father who stood up when I went to the ladies' room and who held out my chair when I came back to the dinner table. I knew I had to marry him; he was exactly like my dad, and they just don't make 'em that way anymore.

TONY GOLDWYN

Actor and director who has appeared in numerous films, ranging from The Last Samurai *to* Ghost. *His directing credits include* A Walk on the Moon *and* Someone Like You. *Onstage, Tony has been seen at Circle in the Square, Second Stage Theatre, Vineyard Theatre, Manhattan Theatre Club, and the Williamstown Theatre Festival, to name a few.*

THE SMELL OF FISH WAS overpowering. I could tell that Pop was starting to turn green at the gills himself, but in my narcissistic six-year-old view of the world, I felt no sympathy for him—only excitement at stepping aboard a real boat at eleven o'clock at night (a part of the circadian cycle that had eluded me thus far in the summer of 1966). On the San Diego docks, a few of the larger commercial fishing boats were preparing for work. The noise of winches turning and men shouting filled the air. The idea that people were just going to work at this hour seemed exotic in the extreme. Our boat was considerably smaller than her neighbors, a weather-beaten sportfisher substantially beyond her prime. To me, of course, she was glorious.

As we set out to sea, my Pop—Sam Goldwyn, Jr.—tucked me into my berth and instructed me to get a good night's sleep so that I'd be fit for the tuna we were going to engage in battle at dawn. Lying in the musty sheets three feet from my father—all six feet four inches of him crammed into his berth—and certain that sleep was not the merest possibility, I quickly slipped into oblivion, lulled by the swelling sea and the chug of the engine carrying us out to the edge of the Pacific Shelf.

I awoke to the noise of retching. My poor dad's legs were sticking out of the tiny head, his stomach apparently turned inside out. It was still dark and, leaving Pop to his suffering, I ran up onto the deck where the captain and the first mate were drinking coffee, smoking cigarettes, and preparing the rods. Ready for action, oblivious to my grumbling stomach, and not yet having developed my future dependence on caffeine, I had a line in the water within minutes and patiently waited for a silver monster to take my lure. I didn't have to wait long. Within thirty seconds, the line went taut and the reel started to scream—a noise that hardly compared to the shriek that emanated from me.

The first mate (let's call him Danny) rammed my fishing rod into its stay and set the hook. He coached me through the process of wrestling the invisible behemoth into submission. After fifteen minutes of sustained screaming from me, and a couple of spectacular leaps out of the water from my adversary, we at last had a four-foot-long albacore (okay, maybe three) flopping about on the deck. Still yelling my head off, I ran below and began to violently shake my poor sick father. "Pop! Pop! I caught a fish! I caught a fish!" Dutiful as ever, Pop dragged himself up the stairs and, the first light of morning blinding his swollen eyes, grabbed his camera while I held my foe by the tail. (Not much bigger than the fish myself, I'd managed to hoist him into a vertical position with the assistance of Danny.)

Within an hour, three more fat fish lay on the deck, and my voice was hoarse from screeching. While Pop was still far too ill to hold up a rod of his own, he dutifully snapped a photo of each catch. Sometime after 7 a.m., it suddenly struck me that I hadn't had breakfast. The rod was abandoned, and the captain whipped up some eggs on toast. About four seconds after my breakfast went down, it powered its way right back up again in a textbook display of projectile vomiting. I was not to be spared my father's affliction.

Undeterred, I spent the remainder of the morning alternately barfing on the deck—or overboard, when possible— and reeling in sea monsters. The state of my tummy eventually improved. My father's did not. By sundown, we were back at the dock in San Diego with seven or eight enormous albacore. The fish were traded to the local cannery for ten cases of canned tuna. The idea of exchanging a few dead fish for a lifetime supply of tuna sandwiches was yet another miracle of my young life.

When I recall my father's face that day, I see a strange combination of pain and radiance. Until I had children of my own, I never could have grasped what lay beneath his expression. However close to succumbing from his nausea, he was fairly overcome with joy at witnessing my elation. I've since learned that one of life's sublime delights is to watch one's offspring experience the ecstasy of discovery. (Sadly, that feeling is inversely proportional to the anguish of watching them endure pain.) My parents had separated earlier that year, and my father was surely going through a period of absolute torture. Nevertheless, in our eighteen hours together on that boat (without any of my three siblings), he managed to give me what remains a pristine memory of happiness and connection to him.

AL ROKER

Co-anchor, weather reporter, the Today *show.*

FOR *BIG SHOES,* I INTERVIEWED men and women about their fathers. I talked to men about being fathers and what fatherhood means to them. It was a piece of cake. Ask them about their fathers and the floodgates opened; the words came pouring out. Ask them about being a father and you couldn't shut 'em up.

As long as I was talking about other people's fathers, I was okay. Yet every time I sat down to write about my own experience of being a father and exploring what my dad meant to me, I had trouble. This wasn't the "writer's block" you hear so much about; it was more like a deep freeze. I wasn't sure what to do.

Should my essay be a lighthearted paean to fatherhood? Should I tell some cute stories about my kids? Share some warm memories of my late father and provide some thoughtful insights into the state of fatherhood today?

I knew I could do all that. What brought me up short was writing about my father. He died more than three years ago, and it's difficult to write about it. I can talk about his being gone much more easily than I can write about it. Maybe because I have to really think about it. Think about all he meant to me. Think about how much I miss him. Think about never seeing him again.

It is a pain more real than I could ever have imagined. You see, it never crossed my mind that he would die. It's silly, I know, but it just never dawned on me. He was always there.

Then, just after July 4, 2001, my sister Alisa called to tell me that there was a problem with one of Dad's X-rays during a routine physical. His diaphragm was elevated. On further inspection there seemed to be a tumor in his lung. Tiny, really.

When I asked him about it, he answered with his typical nonchalance. "Hey, man. It's nuthin'. No big deal!" But I knew better. He blew it off too quickly. He was a man who didn't dwell on unpleasantness and he was quick to dismiss illness. He had lost his father, his mother, and his sister to cancer. It was something that frightened him. And my father was not a man easily frightened.

He grew up first in Freeport, Long Island, then Jamaica, Queens. He hung around with high school thugs with nicknames like "Dead-Eye" and "Jelly Roll." He had his share of rumbles and fights. He was, by his own admission, a "badass."

But all that ended, he once told me, when he saw a girl with, and I'm quoting now, "the cutest butt he had ever seen" hanging it out while she was washing windows at her mother's house one

Saturday morning. He just happened to be rolling by on his motorcycle. Paying more attention to my future mother's tush than to the road, he suddenly came face-to-face with a truck that had driven into his path. My dad, to avoid a crash, laid down his motorcycle and slid under the truck. Talk about a guy doing anything to get noticed by a girl.

Well, it worked. They started dating, and right after Isabel Bernadette Smith graduated from John Adams High School, Albert Lincoln Roker married her. Soon she got pregnant, and this carefree guy had a family on the way.

As a young man, he demonstrated real artistic ability. He worked for the Ideal Toy Company, designing box art for their toys. But prevailing prejudice of the day kept him from being able to join the commercial artists' union. So with a new baby and a wife to take care of, he got a job driving a bus. To make ends meet, he sold his beloved motorcycle.

I always remembered that sacrifice he made for my mom and me, selling that bike. A year before he died, before I knew there was a tumor eating away at him, I got him a car. He had always wanted a Lincoln LS. I brought him to the dealer, ostensibly to get his advice on a van I wanted for my production company. There, on the showroom floor, was a champagne-colored Lincoln LS. As we walked by it, I said, "Now that's sweet. Maybe we should take it for a spin?" He stopped and admired it and said, "Noooo. Little too rich for my blood." I looked at him and replied, "Well, you're gonna have to, seeing as how these keys are yours."

With that, I tossed him the car keys. He caught them,

looked at me, looked at the car, then back at me. This time, he had tears in his eyes. As the dealer went over the car with him, he kept shaking his head and hugging me. He was so happy and grateful, yet it was his belief in me, his insistence that his kids could be whatever they wanted to be, that put me where I am. His influence gave me the confidence to pursue my career. So, in a way, he was the one who purchased that car.

So here's my dilemma: Most people are expecting something funny from me. I would like to write something funny. But I can't. The sense of loss is overwhelming. A lot of the people in this book have fathers who are still alive, and in talking to some of them, a feeling of jealousy would come over me as they spoke about their dads. The unfairness of it all would wash over me and I would find myself getting sad all over again.

From those whose fathers had passed away, I was hoping to glean some nugget, some idea of what to do with the hole in my heart that my father's death had left. How did they move on with their lives? I talked with Matt Lauer, who also lost his father several years ago to cancer. He told me there are still days when something happens and he reaches for the phone to call his dad about it. It brings him up short. I can relate to that.

My father's lung cancer was officially diagnosed in August of 2001. He missed his first chemotherapy treatment on September 11, 2001. I felt gypped. Here's this all-consuming tragedy in my life, but how could I feel terrible about it when the nation was grieving, shocked and numbed by the unspeakable horror of September 11? In a way, it was a blessing. No one could possibly know how bad I was feeling because as a country we were all hurting.

On October 3, my dad collapsed during a chemotherapy session and was admitted to the hospital. For the next three weeks, I visited him at Memorial Sloan-Kettering Cancer Center before the *Today* show to sit with him for about an hour. Then I'd head over to Studio 1-A and get ready for the program. Invariably, I would go into one of our dressing rooms, close the door, and cry for about ten minutes. Then I'd slap some Visine in my eyes and put on a happy face.

It was the lowest I have ever felt. And yet I had to continue my day-to-day life. People don't tune in to the *Today* show to watch a morose weatherman. "Say, folks, the weather is just about as bad as I feel." Or how about, "Where are you all from? Yeah, well, at least your father's not lying in a cancer ward dying!"

And yet, he was still my father. One morning, despite my best efforts to keep a stiff upper lip, I started to cry. He held my hand and said in a whispery voice that still had remnants of strength and steel in it, "C'mon, son. Don't cry. Please. I've been married to the same woman for almost fifty years. I have six great kids and a bunch of wonderful grandkids. Wish I had me some more time, but it's been a really good life. I got nuthin' to kick about."

He's the guy who's dying and he's comforting me. That's what being a father is all about. It's making sure your children are taken care of. Because you love them more than you love yourself. You take enormous pride in what your children do, even if it surpasses what you do.

My first television job was as the weekend weatherman in Syracuse, New York, at WHEN-TV. It was 1974 and my father was still driving a New York City Transit Authority bus. The station had business cards printed up for me. Now, what the heck was I supposed to do with business cards? I took a bunch home with me for a visit, showed them to Mom and Dad, and inadvertently left them on my dad's dresser.

Fast-forward a few months. I'm sitting in the newsroom and I get a call from some guy who lives in Brooklyn. He's passing through Syracuse and wanted to say hi. A day or two later, the same thing happens again: Some stranger from Brooklyn calls to say hello and tells me to keep up the good work. This goes on for a few weeks, one or two calls each week. Finally, I ask a caller how she got my number. The woman answers, "I ride on your father's bus. He's been handing out your business cards to all us riders, telling us to call you for support!"

Six days before he died, he was transferred to Calvary Hospital, a wonderful place in the Bronx. It is the nation's only palliative care hospital. You go there when cancer has robbed you of any possibility of survival. You are treated with dignity, respect, and love. Medical problems are all dealt with, and your family can come and spend those remaining days without worry.

For six days, my mom and brother and sisters and I camped out in my father's hospital room as his life slowly ebbed. His speech was gone but his eyes were still alive and communicating. We sat, talked, laughed, and cried. Dr. Michael Brescia, the director of the hospital, told me that he would come into our room at the end of a hard day and that the love for my father washed over and rejuvenated him.

The doctors treating him were amazed at how my father clung to life. One doctor pulled me aside and told me that he felt my father was hanging on because of my mother. "He needs to know it's okay to go." So I had a very difficult conversation with my mother. "Mom," I began, "you have to tell Dad it's okay to go. You have to tell him you'll be all right." She took it all in, got up, and walked into his room. I watched as she leaned over the man she had been married to for almost fifty years and told him, "Albert, if this is what you want to do, it's okay. If you need to go, you go." I chuckled to myself. It was almost like, "If you have to go play cards with the boys, don't worry about me."

Yet he hung on for another day and a half. Around 2 a.m. on October 30, I sent my brother Chris home. My mother was asleep on a cot next to Dad's bed. I held his hand and looked at him. "Dad, if you're going to go, you gotta go now while she's asleep." I was crying as I talked to him. "She's not going to let go, so you go now. I'm going to be right here." He just kept looking at me; his breathing was hard, chugging like a train, his hand in mine. "You know Chris and I will take care of Mom, so there's nothing to worry about. So I'll just sit here."

I held his hand for the better part of an hour. His eyes closed and he grew quiet. He was gone. I sat there with him for another fifteen minutes and just looked at him. He looked like a baby lying there. I will never forget the way his face looked that night.

I discovered so much about my father in the days following

his death. He never really talked about work that much, especially his bus driver days. He drove a bus to put food on the table. In fact, while he was a driver, he was literally putting food on the table. To make extra cash, he and a couple of buddies opened up a lunchroom at the depot, serving sandwiches and hot entrees. It got so popular, he and his pals were given better driving shifts so that they would be around to make lunch. Maybe that's where I got my love of food. Here was this blue-collar guy who loved to cook, before it was cool for men other than chefs to cook.

But we all knew Dad wanted to be a dispatcher. It was the next rung up on the NYC Transit Authority ladder. More pay, better benefits, better hours. He would do anything to improve his family's lot in life. If that meant starting at the lower end of another position that paid more, he'd do it. Standing outside, in all kinds of weather, making sure the buses were on schedule, the dispatcher keeps the lifeblood of a bus system flowing.

To achieve his dream, he studied and he studied and he studied. And after twelve years as a bus driver, he became a dispatcher. But that wasn't enough. He then became a chief dispatcher. Eventually, he was recruited to join management as a labor relations person. This union guy was now on the other side of the table. He had been with the NYC Transit in one form or another for almost thirty years when he retired in 1990.

Before, during, and after his funeral, I found out how many people he had touched, how many lives he had changed. Men and women came up to tell me how he had mentored them, nurtured them, and helped them both professionally and personally.

One man told me about the time my dad saved his career. It

seems the guy had been drinking and showed up drunk for his shift. My father pulled him aside and told him, in a voice that he says "scared the crap out of me, yet never went above a whisper," he was to take his bus out, drive to the end of his route, and call the bus in broken down. He told him to drink plenty of hot coffee and wait for a tow truck.

My father told the man that if he ever showed up drunk again, he'd have him brought up on charges and fired. The man told me he walked the straight and narrow the rest of his career. With tears in his eyes, he said that Dad saved his job, his family, and his life.

I heard story after story about my father affecting people in ways big and small. I felt bad that I never knew that side of him while he was alive. It shouldn't have surprised me, yet to me, he was just "Dad." I never really thought about him other than that he was a terrific father and grandfather. His grandkids adored "Pop-Pop." My mother was so great at giving each grandchild something that she thought they would cherish of his, whether it was one of his beloved fishing poles or a sweatshirt or his ever-present baseball cap.

I know that I have tried to fill his "Big Shoes" as a father to my kids. He was a patient guy. Every now and then, he'd lose that patience and break out "The Belt." I was around nine and I remember just before one spanking he trotted out the old bromide, "This is going to hurt me more than it does you." When he said that, I asked him to do us both a favor then and skip the spanking. He started laughing so hard, he sat down and said, "Get outta here, and don't tell your mother."

When I'm dealing with my children, after a long day, I think about him. Eight hours driving a bus, dealing with New Yorkers, making change and small talk, *then* coming home and dealing with six kids and a wife who had been cooped up with those kids. Yet he played with us, talked to us, and listened to us. His was a rare gift. He would listen.

I know my eighteen-year-old daughter, Courtney, wishes I could master that art. It's something I'm trying to do. I'm trying to resist the urge to dispense pearls of wisdom. Sometimes, your kids just want to talk. Not be lectured or preached to. Dad didn't do a lot of preaching. He let you figure it out and then would just nod, pat you on the knee, and walk away.

We became even closer when I became a father myself. Everything he did, everything he said suddenly made sense the second I was responsible for a child. It was the moment I first held my child. I remember the first time I held my daughter Courtney in my arms. Courtney's mother and her son and I were standing in the office of an upstate New York child welfare agency. Our caseworker walked in holding this small brown face wrapped in a pink blanket. She handed Alice Roker this precious bundle. Alice held her for a while and then handed her to me. It was the first time I experienced love at first sight. And fear. And terror. And hope. In other words, I was a father.

Courtney's mother and I would divorce, but the bond of parenthood will always keep us linked to a power greater than ourselves. Our child. I would get to experience that feeling twice more. Deborah Roberts gave me the gift of seeing my second girl born. On November 17, 1998, I became a father again. It may be trite, cliché, or corny, but watching this miracle called birth from conception to delivery is amazing. I felt my life change again. Leila Ruth Roker was born, and again I felt this kinship with my father. I watched him holding his new granddaughter in his arms. I recalled him telling me countless times, "I remember when I could hold you in one hand." How many times would I tell Leila that?

Then in November 2001, two weeks after my father died, we found out we were pregnant again. This time, as we did the first, we used in vitro fertilization to get pregnant. However, this time a new procedure allowed the doctors to tell us, in addition to any genetic problems with the fetus, whether it would be a boy or a girl. Unlike with Leila, we found out this baby's sex before it was implanted. It was a girl.

Hey, would I have liked a boy? Sure. But this was good, too. Another baby in the family. Of course, my dad would've loved to see a Roker grandson, but it was not to be.

We decided not to do amniocentesis since there was a risk of miscarriage given Deborah was forty-two, and if it had been a Down's syndrome baby, we would have kept her anyway. So when it was time to do our twenty-week sonogram, we held our breath as the doctor performed the procedure. Deborah, watching the screen, asked the doctor what that protrusion was. "Well, I don't know who told you this is a girl, but you're having a boy!" he proclaimed.

A boy? A boy? A BOY!!!! I was speechless. Deborah had a

hundred questions. It seems the test, with its 90 percent accuracy, was wrong. We were going to have a boy. There were questions as to what went wrong, but my mother had the answer. "Your father did it!" she exclaimed. "Your father went to God and worked out a deal." Yep, one last labor negotiation.

Upon hearing this theory of my mother's, Deborah said to me, "You don't believe that, do you?" "Hey, who knows?" I answered. I like the whole idea. I know he would.

On July 18, 2002, Nicholas Albert Roker was born. While the doctors focused on Deborah following her Cesarean delivery, I was in our room with Nicholas, alone. I was holding him and started to cry. As I read over this, I realize I cry a lot. I think Arnold Schwarzenegger would categorize me as a girly man. I was crying for a few reasons. I was happy about the birth of this little boy. I was thrilled to have a son. And I was missing my father until I realized Nicky looked just like him in those final moments after he passed away.

And during the nights afterward, in the light between night and morning, when I would hold my son and look at his face, I saw my father. I found a way to fill those "Big Shoes." My boy is filling them. My daughters are filling them. I watch them growing up and realize they're the ones who walk in his footsteps. My job is to make sure they keep walking.

ACKNOWLEDGMENTS

I'D LIKE TO THANK AND ACKNOWLEDGE the following people:

Amy Rennert, the conductor who kept this love train chugging even when yours truly would get off track. Alfred Geller and Laura Sher of Geller Media Management for their constant help and guidance. Jennifer Weinberg of Al Roker Productions for her gentle prodding to get this labor of love finished. To all the people who sat still for interviews without whom this book would not have been possible. And to all the fathers out there, thanks for being there. Without you, there's nobody to read this book.

—*Al Roker*

The greatest pleasure of editing *Big Shoes* is that the interviews I've done with contributors have led me to remember so many wonderful stories about my own childhood and the profound influence my father, Irwin Rennert, continues to have on my life. Like many *Big Shoes* contributors, I find that my dad teaches me most by example. From him, I have learned the meaning of loyalty, honesty, and hard work, as well as the art of conversation and negotiation. What wasn't learned was inherited: my sense of humor, for example. I still turn to him for guidance and his advice is always sound. He ends many conversations by calling me "kid," and the affection in that tugs at my heart.

I dedicate this book to him.

Although this is a book about fathers and fatherhood, my mom deserves credit, too, for, well, for everything.

Pamela Feinsilber's editorial skills and experience helped make this book better. My associate Dena Fischer provided much input throughout the entire process. She also introduced me to Susan Abramson, who has the best Rolodex in the business.

Bob Miller embraced the idea for this book from the start. Thanks also to the rest of the Hyperion team, including Leslie Wells, Will Schwalbe, Ellen Archer, and Elisa Lee.

I had the great good fortune to work with the amazing Al Roker. I am grateful to him and to the many *Big Shoes* contributors for sharing their very intimate and revealing stories in print and conversation.

I am most thankful in work and in life to Louise Kollenbaum, an accomplished artist and writer, who inspires me daily. She sets her standards high and with great integrity. I didn't get to know her father, John Kollenbaum, but she tells me that much of the best of her comes from him.

—*Amy Rennert*